PROMISES—NOT MY WILL

BOOK THREE

Stephanie Fleming
Shelly Funk

New Harbor Press

RAPID CITY, SD

Funk & Fleming/New Harbor Press
1601 Mt.Rushmore Rd, Ste 3288
Rapid City, SD 57701
www.newharborpress.com

Promises - Not My Will, Book II / Stephanie Fleming & Shelly Funk -- 1st ed.
ISBN 978-1-63357-478-6

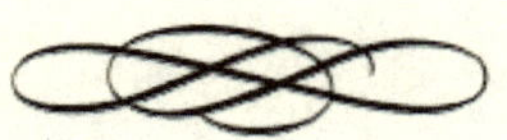

CHAPTER ONE

Jexi stood in front of the full-length mirror evaluating her dress. It was Valentine's Day and the church's school was holding a dance. Hunter and Jexi had agreed to be chaperones for the evening along with Ben and Shaya. It was Shaya's first year as the principal, so this event was important. The dance was organized as a fundraiser for the school and would hopefully attract a large crowd.

Jexi wore a bright red maxi dress with short sleeves and a V-neck. It was simple, but that was Jexi's style. While she never had been the frilly girl type, she loved how the dress flared when she spun in a circle. Her cross necklace draped her neck, and she wore gold teardrop earrings that Shaya's family had given her for Christmas. Even her makeup was understated, just giving a hint of color to her eyes, cheeks, and lips. Satisfied with her appearance, she gave one last swish of the dress skirt. Hunter would be there soon, so she spritzed some perfume and gathered her purse.

As if on cue, there was a knock at the door. She waltzed to answer, feeling blissful as she anticipated seeing him. He still gave her butterflies, even after all these months. If she was honest with herself, she never remembered feeling this way with Brennan. It made her sad to think she almost married someone without knowing this feeling. She and Hunter had grown even closer since their return from Honduras, and she smiled as she opened the door.

Hunter gasped softly. "You look stunning!" he said, almost in a whisper. Jexi giggled internally, thinking that she might have taken his breath away. She spun in a circle to show off.

"This ole' thing?" she asked playfully, as she tugged up one corner of her skirt. "It's nothing."

Hunter shook his head. "No, it's a lot more than nothing. You are absolutely beautiful." He leaned in to kiss her cheek.

"Thanks," Jexi said, blushing just a little. "You look pretty stunning yourself!"

He held out a bouquet of flowers and a box of chocolate-covered strawberries. "I almost forgot. These are for you," he said.

"Aww, they are beautiful," Jexi said as she smelled the heavenly aroma of the flowers. "My favorite, lilies! You remembered!"

Jexi rushed to put the flowers in water and the strawberries in the fridge. "I'm all ready," she said to Hunter.

Hunter held out his arm, and they went to the car. He held the door open for her and made sure she was in before shutting the door. He did that for her every time they got in the car. Jexi never could remember Brennan doing that for her. She felt so blessed. They talked nonstop on their way to the school and arrived sooner than Jexi would have liked. She wished they could have some more time alone.

Shaya saw Jexi and Hunter walk in and rush over to them. "I'm so glad you guys are here! I have something to show you." She grabbed Jexi's hand and tugged her along. "You look beautiful, by the way," Shaya said over her shoulder.

Jexi looked at Shaya and whistled. "So do you!" she said, almost stumbling. "Slow down, would ya?"

They entered the gym and Jexi saw instantly where Shaya was taking her. Jexi screamed across the room, "MOM, DAD!" and ran toward her parents. She hugged them both and then stood back. "What are you doing here?" she asked.

"We just decided to drop in for a visit on our way back to Kansas City," her dad answered. "Your mom remembered you telling her about this dance, and we figured it would be a perfect time to come see you."

Jexi smiled. "I'm so glad you did! I've missed you so much!" She hugged them again. At once, she stood straight. "You have to meet Hunter!"

"We'd love to, dear!" said her mother. "Oh honey, you look so beautiful!"

"Thanks, Mom," Jexi said. She looked up and saw Hunter and Ben walking into the gym. She waved them over. When they approached, she introduced everyone. "Mom, Dad, this is Hunter, and this is Ben. Guys, these are my parents, Louise and Gary."

Everyone shook hands and muttered pleasantries such as *"How do you do?"* and *"Nice to meet you."*

Louise looked at Hunter and asked, "Have you been taking care of our girl?"

Jexi blushed, "Moooom," she whined.

Hunter laughed. "It's alright, Jexi." He winked at her. "I understand why she's asking." He turned to Louise. "I do the best I can, Ma'am. I really do care for her quite a bit."

Jexi noticed Shaya flutter by. She watched her friend in her element and smiled at herself. Shaya had found her passion in her job at the school. She greeted students and their families as they entered in a way that was natural for her. One would never guess she was an introvert, the way she shone in this moment.

Jexi liked the dress Shaya was wearing. It was a brilliant blue that brought out the color in her eyes. It fit her perfectly but modestly and draped to the floor. There were small rhinestones placed at the collar of the square neck and around the hem. Shaya seemed to be glowing tonight.

The entire town must have been in attendance because the gym was packed to capacity. The night continued to run smoothly. Jexi danced with her parents and Hunter and laughed so much her side hurt. "Let's take a walk," Hunter whispered to her. "I need some air."

They held hands as they returned from outside. Walking back into the gym, they noticed a table stacked with Valentine's Day trinkets and toys. Jexi giggled as she looked at the items available. "Oh look," she said. "This necklace is to die for!" She held up a gold plastic chain, adorned with a giant pretend gemstone. She put the necklace back onto the table. "Oh dear! They even have gorgeous diamond rings."

Hunter picked up one of the oversized plastic rings. He laughed as he placed the ring on her finger. "Please take this ring as a token of my affection. I'd love for you to marry me, my dear," he said as they chuckled together.

Jexi tossed her head back with laughter. "How could I decline such an elegant gem? Of course, my darling, my answer is yes." She linked her arm to his and pretended to do the wedding march humming the song aloud. "Look at us," she said in a goofy manner, "We are married."

Hunter stopped abruptly and spun her to face him. He had stopped laughing and looked very serious. "Jexi," he said.

Jexi stood still. "What's wrong?" she asked. She wondered if she had offended him with her teasing.

"What if I'm not joking?" Hunter asked.

"Wha . . . what?" Jexi asked, stunned.

"What if I'm not joking?" Hunter repeated. "What if I really want to marry you?"

"You mean for real?" Jexi asked. "Like for real, for real?"

"Yes," Hunter said. "Let's face it, you already know that I love you."

Jexi caught her breath. She could see in his eyes that he was serious. She thought back to the first time he'd told her he loved her. She knew how he felt. She loved him too, and she'd allowed herself to admit it to him. She stood in stunned silence for a full thirty seconds, although it seemed like an eternity. She could see fear starting to show on his face. "So, did you just propose to me?"

Hunter smiled. "I think I did. What do you say? I love you and want to be with you forever. Marry me, Jexi."

Jexi smiled back. "What else can I say? It has to be yes, Hunter. It has to be yes!" She held out her hand that supported the gaudy fake ring. "And the ring is perfect!" she added with a laugh.

Hunter's face became serious. "I am going to replace that with a real ring," he said.

"But can I keep this one, too?" Jexi asked.

Hunter couldn't help but laugh. "Whatever you want," he replied. "That will be a reminder of this fantastic night."

CHAPTER TWO

Hunter and Jexi went to find their friends and Jexi's parents. They gathered them together to announce their engagement. Jexi held out her hand with the goofy ring on it. There was laughter, and then her father said, "Nice ring, Hunter! Did you find it in a Cracker Jack box?"

Shaya rolled her eyes. "Good one, you two," she said. "You had me going there for a moment."

Hunter chuckled. "Well, I admit that this wasn't planned and this won't be her real ring, but we really did get engaged tonight."

Shaya's jaw fell open. "Seriously?!" she shrieked.

Jexi's eyes teared up. "Seriously!" she squealed back.

Instantly, the realization set in and there were shouts of congratulations and well wishes from everyone. Jexi looked at Shaya and saw her sniffling and wiping away tears.

"What's wrong?" Jexi asked. "I thought you would be happy for me."

Shaya blew her nose on a tissue and looked at her best friend. "I am," she said. "These are happy tears."

Jexi looked skeptical. "Um, you sure about that?"

Shaya nodded. "Can we go somewhere private to talk?" she asked.

"You're scaring me, Shay," Jexi said. "Are you sure you are okay?"

Shaya pulled Jexi to a corner of the gym. "I'm so very okay," she said. "I hadn't planned to tell you yet, but I have news of my own tonight. I was waiting for the right moment to share with you. Now seems as good a time as any." She paused and wiped away more tears. "Ben and I are going to have a baby!"

It was Jexi's turn to jump and shriek. "Woohoo!" she yelled. She enveloped her friend in a hug. "Best night, ever," she whispered in Shaya's ear.

Shaya smiled. "I am so excited," she said. "But do me a favor and don't say anything to anyone yet. I'm only about eight weeks along. We kind of want to hold off until the end of the first trimester."

"I won't," Jexi promised. "But can I at least tell Hunter?"

Shaya nodded. "But no one else, okay?"

"I promise. God has given us so much to celebrate," Jexi said. "I am amazed at His goodness, every time!"

The girls made their way back to the dance and spent the rest of the evening laughing, enjoying their families, and dreaming of their futures.

The Sunday after the dance, the group gathered for their monthly video chat with some of their dear friends from Aldea Gracia, Honduras. Over time, they had formed a deep bond with the villagers, especially Juan Carlos Sr., his wife Angelica, and their seven children. Since returning from their mission trip, where they had helped rescue Juan Carlos from his captor and supported the village in preserving their land, these virtual reunions had become a source of joy and encouragement. They cherished every update and glimpse into the lives of the people they had come to love.

Aunt Jessie pressed the phone number into the tablet and waited. Juan Carlos answered on the second ring. "Hola, Jessie!" he exclaimed. *"Mi amiga! Como estas?* How are you?"

"We are well, Juan Carlos!" Jessie answered. "How are things in Aldea Gracia? How are Angelica and baby Carmen?"

"Little Carmen is growing so fast," Juan Carlos said in his broken English. He looked over his shoulder, *"Mamacita,* bring Carmen to show our friends." He looked back at the screen, beaming proudly. "She needed a diaper change."

A chorus of delighted *"ooohs"* and *"aaahs"* filled the room as the baby's face appeared on the screen. At just three months old, little Carmen was irresistibly chubby and utterly adorable.

Jexi glanced at Shaya and noticed she was wiping away tears. She subtly reached over and squeezed her friend's hand.

"How is everyone else in the village?" Aunt Jessie asked. "Are JC and Maya doing well?" She recalled the pictures of the Christmas Eve wedding that had been sent to the States.

"Oh, yes," Juan Carlos replied. "They are very happy to be married. They share a lot of love. We think Carlita will marry soon. Antonio has asked us for permission but has not asked her yet. Carlita has been taking classes to become a nurse. She wishes to practice medicine in our little village."

Jexi shoved her ringed hand in front of everyone. "Hunter and I are getting married too!"

Juan Carlos laughed. "Oh, what a ring you have. So . . . pretty."

Hunter sheepishly informed him that it was just a fill-in until he could get the ring he actually wanted for Jexi. "She keeps showing that monstrosity to everyone."

Juan Carlos nodded in understanding, still laughing.

Aunt Jessie spoke again. "We miss you all," she told Juan Carlos. "We are trying to plan another trip to see you soon. We just don't know when we can come down yet. Especially now that we have a wedding to plan."

"We understand," Juan Carlos replied. "You are always welcome in our little village, whenever you can come. How is your new job, Jessie? How do you like being settled?"

"It took some getting used to," Jessie admitted. "But I do love being the counselor at the Christian school. I enjoy working with the students."

"I am glad," Juan Carlos said. "Angelica would like to greet you all."

Angelica appeared on the screen. "Hello, everyone," she said.

Everyone waved. "How are you feeling, Angelica?" asked Jessie.

"Much better, thank you," Angelica answered. "It is nice to be able to get up and move around. Carmen is such a good baby. And since Delfini has taken over the teacher responsibilities at the school, I am feeling much relief."

"Speaking of Delfini," Shaya interjected. "How are she and Andre adjusting to village life?" Andre and Delfini had moved their family to the village after the rescue of Juan Carlos. Shaya was concerned that it would be difficult for the village to accept them since Andre had held Juan Carlos captive. She prayed everyone would be as forgiving as Juan Carlos had been.

Angelica smiled. "They are doing so well," she said. "Andre still apologizes for keeping Juan Carlos held captive, but we tell him every time that he is forgiven. We love them so much. Andre went to Choluteca and took classes to become an ordained minister! We are very proud of him. His wife and children have also accepted Jesus, and we have wonderful church services every week. Andre is a very skilled minister."

Juan Carlos came back onto the screen. "Senor Hunter, gracias for the beautiful guitars you have sent to the boys. They practice every day. I have to make them stop playing to do their chores!" He laughed.

Jexi looked at Hunter, and he blushed. "I didn't know you sent them guitars!" she said, squeezing his hand.

"It's not a big deal," Hunter said. "I just knew those rickety ones we built wouldn't last very long, so I wanted them to have something real to play."

Jexi's heart swelled. She didn't think she could have loved him more than she did when he proposed, but she was wrong. She marveled at the fact she was going to marry such a wonderful person and spend the rest of her life falling more and more in love.

Jessie asked Juan Carlos about the trial concerning Mr. McGreggor, the owner of the land surrounding Aldea Gracia. "Any news?" she inquired. "Do you know when you go to court?"

Juan Carlos shook his head. "No, not yet," he said. "The government wants to press charges against Mr. McGreggor, but cannot, until the case is settled in the United States. I pray for him every day."

McGreggor had tried illegal means to kick the villagers out of their home but failed. Jessie was proud to be part of the group who put a stop to his hijinks.

Jessie nodded, "You have the heart of Jesus, Juan Carlos."

CHAPTER THREE

Shaya and Ben woke up early and eagerly prepared for their second doctor visit and first ultrasound since discovering they were pregnant. They couldn't wait to hear the baby's heartbeat and see the black-and-white image of their baby. They had planned to meet with Shaya's family for dinner tonight to announce their news. It had been a hard secret to keep, but they felt it was best.

They sat in the waiting room, listening for Shaya's name to be called. When it was, they followed the nurse back to an exam room. Shaya undressed, slipped on the hospital gown, and took her place on the exam table.

The nurse returned and began setting up the ultrasound machine. "This might feel a little cold," she warned Shaya with a gentle smile, before squeezing a bit of clear gel onto her abdomen. With practiced hands, she guided the wand across Shaya's stomach, carefully searching for the baby's heartbeat.

The nurse was silent for what seemed like forever. She moved the wand all over Shaya's belly, pressing and listening. Shaya was listening as well but wasn't sure what she was supposed to be hearing. The nurse looked at Shaya and Ben while she replaced the wand on the machine. "I'll be right back," she said quietly.

Ben and Shaya exchanged glances. "What do you suppose that's about?" Shaya asked.

"I don't know," Ben replied.

"You don't think something is wrong, do you?" Shaya posed with worry in her voice.

"Stay calm," Ben said, trying to comfort her. "I'm sure everything is fine."

After a moment, the nurse returned with the doctor in tow. The doctor said hello to the couple and immediately applied more gel to Shaya's tummy and started the ultrasound again.

His mouth grimaced into a frown as he began to speak. "I'm sorry, but we are having difficulty locating your baby's heartbeat," he announced. "He pressed the wand into one spot and pointed to the screen. "This white spot is your baby." Shaya's eyes filled with tears as she looked at Ben. "We are going to do an exam."

Ben's face was grim. "What does this mean, doctor? What's wrong with the baby? What is happening?"

"It could mean nothing," the doctor replied, "Or it could mean that Shaya is miscarrying."

Shaya let out a small yelp. "Mis . . . mis . . . miscarrying?" she stammered. "I haven't had any pain or anything! It's a mistake, right?"

"We hope so," the doctor answered. "The exam will let us know for sure."

While they had been talking, the nurse had already gotten out all the supplies needed for the exam and was ready for the doctor to begin. There was silence in the room as he conducted the procedure. When he finished, he removed his gloves, washed his hands, and stood next to Shaya, across from Ben. "I'm sorry, your body is in the process of a miscarriage. You haven't had symptoms yet, but you will soon."

Shaya began to cry. Ben wrapped his arms around her, and he was shedding tears as well. He looked at the doctor. "Isn't there anything we can do?" he asked desperately.

"Unfortunately, there is not," answered the doctor. "Shaya, go ahead and get dressed. I have more information to share, but I want you to be more comfortable. The position you are in is far from comfortable. I will be back in a few minutes."

Shaya's mind was numb, wrapped in a haze of disbelief. Tears streamed down her face, but the doctor's words felt distant, muffled by the fog surrounding her thoughts. *Her baby was gone. How can this be? God, where are You?* she cried silently. *You've never failed me before . . . what is happening?*

Moving on autopilot, she dressed slowly, her hands trembling. Then she and Ben sank into the available chairs, sitting in heavy silence as they waited for the doctor to return, grieving, broken, and still trying to grasp the weight of what they'd just heard.

Ben spoke first. "We should pray," he said softly.

Shaya spun to look at him. "Pray for what?" she snapped. "Our baby is gone, Ben. What exactly do you suggest we pray for?"

Ben was taken aback at her attitude, although he knew this had to be difficult for her. "God never leaves us, Shay. He is with us even now. We need to turn to Him."

"Easy for you to say," Shaya said through her tears.

"There is nothing easy about this. Don't you think I am devastated too? But" Ben said. "We go to Him no matter what, remember?"

Their conversation was gently interrupted by a soft knock at the door. The doctor stepped in quietly and pulled a stool close to where Shaya and Ben sat.

"First of all," he said, his voice low and compassionate, "I am so very sorry." He looked at each of them with genuine concern before continuing.

"Shaya, during your exam, I discovered that you have a condition called a *septate uterus.* It's a structural issue that not only makes it difficult to conceive, but even more challenging to carry a pregnancy to full term. There simply isn't enough space in the uterus to support a growing baby."

He paused, giving them a moment to absorb the news. "Most pregnancies with this condition, unfortunately, end in miscarriage," he said gently. "I truly wish I had better news."

"Can it be fixed?" Ben asked.

The doctor hesitated. "Yes, it can be surgically corrected, but unfortunately, that type of surgery cannot be considered until a mother has suffered several miscarriages. It isn't something insurance covers because it is a fertility issue."

Shaya sobbed into Ben's shoulder. This just kept getting worse. She feared that her dreams of becoming a mother would never be fulfilled.

The doctor continued with instructions on how to handle the next several days and what to expect from her body. Ben listened carefully, but Shaya didn't hear anything over the screams in her head. She complied when Ben pulled her to her feet and told her it was time to go home. She walked to the car and slid into the passenger seat without saying a word. All she could do was cry. They said nothing to each other for the entire ride.

At the house, she allowed Ben to lead her inside and settle her onto the couch. He fetched a blanket and gently covered her. He kissed her gently on the forehead and told her to rest. She closed her eyes and cried herself to sleep.

Ben stepped outside and called Attie. "Can we get a rain check on dinner? Shaya isn't feeling well."

"What's wrong?" Attie asked. "How can I help? Does she need some soup?"

Ben loved Attie's caring ways, but he just wasn't up to seeing anyone, and he knew Shaya wouldn't be either. "Thanks, Attie," he said, "but she'll be okay. Just a little under the weather. Maybe you can bring some soup by tomorrow. And perhaps you can say an extra prayer for her."

He heard Attie sigh loudly. He knew she was itching to ask more questions, but he was relieved when all she said was, "Okay, I will be by tomorrow evening. Bye, Ben. I love you both."

"We love you too," Ben said. "Goodbye." He ended the call and walked back into the house.

Shaya was soundly asleep. He walked by and gently placed his hand on her shoulder. "Lord, heal her body and her heart. We love You and trust You. We both need You right now, but she needs You more." He continued to the office to sit with his Bible for a while. He wasn't sure what he was going to do, but he knew turning to God would help.

He sat at his desk and stared at his Bible. He didn't even know where to begin, so he just bowed his head and cried. He had never known pain like this before, but he knew he wouldn't survive without his Savior.

CHAPTER FOUR

Shaya woke several hours later. Her neck was slightly sore from lying awkwardly on the couch and she stretched, wincing as she shifted. The house was unnaturally quiet. Too quiet. She looked around the dim room but did not see Ben. For a moment, panic fluttered in her chest before she reminded herself to breathe.

She picked up her cell phone and saw numerous missed calls and text messages; all from Jexi. Guilt pricked at her heart. Jexi had always been persistent, but tonight the messages felt heavier . . . concern layered over concern. She opened the text messaging app and read them one by one, her chest tightening with each line.

By the time she reached the last message, tears blurred her vision. Jexi loved her fiercely. Right now, that love felt like too much to carry.

Shaya glanced at the time stamp on her phone and typed out a quick message back to Jexi, her fingers trembling slightly. She just was not in the mood to talk right now. Not to explain. Not to relive it. *"No, not mad at you. Trust that I will tell you what is going on tomorrow. I'm not up to talking tonight."*

She stared at the screen for a moment after sending it, then turned the phone face down. Tomorrow felt impossibly far away.

She rose slowly and went to look for Ben, padding softly down the hallway. A sliver of light spilled from beneath the office door. She pushed it open and found him there, slumped forward in his chair. He had fallen asleep with his head resting on his Bible at his desk. One hand still clutched the page as if he'd fallen asleep midprayer.

Her heart cracked open.

She watched him sleep for a solid minute, taking in the familiar curve of his shoulders, the lines of exhaustion etched deeper than she'd ever seen. He looked older somehow. Worn. Like grief had physically pressed down on him.

She stepped closer and gently placed her hand on his shoulder, trying not to startle him.

Ben stirred, lifting his head slowly. His eyes were red and swollen, and when he saw her, his composure broke completely. He swiveled his chair around and pulled her down into his lap, holding her like he was afraid she might disappear. They both cried together for a long while with no words, and no restraint. Just shared sorrow spilling freely.

When Shaya finally lifted her head from his shoulder, her voice barely rose above a whisper. "I'm so sorry I lost our baby."

Ben's arms tightened around her instantly. "Shay, this wasn't your fault," he said, his voice thick with emotion. "Please don't ever think that you did anything wrong."

He reached for his Bible with one hand, keeping the other firmly around her waist, grounding them both. "I found a really reassuring verse," he said quietly. "Can I share it with you?"

Shaya nodded, though her heart recoiled slightly. She wasn't angry at God, not exactly, but she felt bruised by Him. Raw. Exposed. She had never imagined she would be in a place where faith felt fragile instead of firm.

Ben began to read, his voice gentle but steady. "The Lord is close to the brokenhearted and saves those who are crushed in spirit. Psalm thirty-four, verse eighteen."

Shaya shook her head, a tear slipping free. "I don't feel Him. It says He's near, but I don't feel Him."

Ben brushed a lock of hair back from her face. "I'm struggling to feel Him too," he admitted. "But I have to believe He's here, despite what I feel. I know in my heart that God will help us through this pain, even if it doesn't look the way we want."

"Ben," Shaya whispered. "What if we can't have any more children because my body is defective?"

The word hung heavy between them.

Ben didn't hesitate. "Your body is not defective," he said firmly. "And we will cross that bridge if we ever come to it. We don't know what God's plan is, but we do know He has one."

He paused, searching her face, then continued softly, "Our role is to pray and to trust. Whatever God's plan holds for us, He will never abandon us. His love for us is unshakable."

"I know that," Shaya said. "It's just hard to have the faith I had yesterday . . . after today."

Suddenly, pain tore through her body and she clutched her stomach, groaning.

The rest of the night blurred into waves of pain and tears. Time lost its meaning. The clock ticked forward but Shaya remained stuck, caught between what had been and what would never be.

Ben stayed with her through it all.

He followed the directions on the medication bottle with care, as if precision alone might protect her. He rubbed her back when the cramps surged, whispered prayers when the sobs returned, and held her hand when words failed completely. When the pain became overwhelming, he didn't rush her or tell her it would pass. He simply stayed.

"What did I do to deserve this torture?" she cried.

Ben turned her toward him, his hands firm and grounding. "You don't deserve this. You are not being punished. Please don't let the enemy convince you otherwise."

Something in his words cut through the fog.

Despite her anger, despite her grief, Shaya felt a faint pull toward God, not away from Him. With what little strength she had left, she whispered, "God, I don't understand this. But I want to trust Your will, not mine. Please ease the physical pain so I can rest."

"And ease the pain in her heart, too, Lord," Ben added. "We trust You."

They said *"Amen"* together, barely audible.

Slowly, almost imperceptibly, the pain began to ease.

When Shaya whispered, "It's working," Ben smiled through tears. "Praise God."

As dawn approached, they moved onto the porch, watching the sky change colors in silence. Shaya leaned into Ben, exhausted but calm.

"A sunrise is a promise of a new beginning," Ben murmured.

Shaya nodded. She didn't know what that new beginning would look like, but for the first time in hours, hope didn't feel impossible.

When Ben later carried her to bed, she clung to him instinctively, her body finally surrendering to sleep.

As he lay beside her, Ben whispered one final prayer, not demanding, not desperate, just honest. Then he pulled her close and let sleep take him too.

Outside, the sun continued to rise. Tomorrow would bring questions and tears, but for now, they were held by each other, and by a God who had not let go.

CHAPTER FIVE

That evening, Ben and Shaya woke to someone knocking on the door and ringing the doorbell. Ben sat up and said, "Oh yeah, I forgot! Your mom is coming over."

"What?!" Shaya shrieked. "My mom? What for?"

Ben explained that he had called Attie to cancel dinner the night before and how he had told her she could visit that evening.

Shaya sat up. "Okay, you go answer the door, I'll change into different clothes real quick."

With the doorbell still ringing, Ben made his way to the front of the house. "I'm coming!" he called.

He opened the door and there stood Attie with a Tupperware container of soup. "What in the world is going on?!" she hollered. "I've been ringing the bell for five minutes! I was about to call 911."

"We fell asleep," Ben explained. "We were up all night." He saw the confusion on Attie's face. "We'll explain in a minute. Come on in."

They walked into the kitchen and Attie put the soup on the counter. "Would you like me to heat this up?" she asked.

Ben nodded. "Yes, please. I'm starving and I'm sure Shay is too."

Once again, Attie showed her confusion, but vented the top of the container and placed it in the microwave. Shaya walked into the kitchen. "Hi, Mom," she said.

One look at her daughter caused Attie to rush to her. "Honey, what happened? What's wrong?" Attie's gaze dropped to Shaya's stomach, and she laid her hand upon her middle. She glanced back up into Shaya's face and watched her daughter crumple into tears.

"Let's all sit down," Ben said. "We need to share something with you."

Everyone sat at the table. Attie was the first to speak. "Is something wrong with the baby?"

Ben gathered his strength to speak. "We had a twelve-week check-up yesterday morning." He took a deep breath. "We found out that the baby has passed, and Shaya is currently miscarrying." Tears began to spill down his face.

Attie's hands shot out to her daughter, and she stood and wrapped her arms around Shaya. "Oh, my sweet girl!" she cried.

The moment stood still and no one spoke for a while. The microwave beeped, but no one moved.

Shaya finally spoke. "Wait. How did you know I was pregnant?"

Attie smiled softly and patted her daughter's cheek. "A mother knows," Attie said.

Shaya hugged her mother. "Mom," she whimpered. "There's more."

Attie sat back down holding Shaya's hands. "You can tell me anything, sweetie," she said. "You know that."

"I might not ever be able to give you grandchildren!" Shaya sobbed.

"Nonsense!" Attie said. "God is bigger than a doctor's words."

"We agree," Ben said, "But Shaya is right. The doctor discovered she has a *septate uterus*. It's a condition where the inside of the uterus is divided by a wall of tissue. While it is possible she can still get pregnant, it makes it much harder for a baby to grow and survive to full term."

Attie sucked in her breath. "Well, fine. I still say God is bigger and He can do miracles. But even if you aren't able to have biological children, there are other ways. Don't you worry. God has a plan for you!"

"Other ways?" Shaya asked. "I'm not ready to think about that right now."

Attie stood again to hug her. "I know, hon, I know. Shhh, shhh, it's okay. One moment at a time."

The microwave beeped again, reminding them that their food was finished. Ben walked over to press the stop button and then returned to the table.

"Mom, I don't want to tell a lot of people," Shaya said. "I know how small towns are and how gossip gets around. Please don't share this with anyone unless we do, okay?"

"Of course," Attie answered. "I'll let you share when and if you are ready. She stood and walked to the cabinets, taking down two bowls. She removed the hot soup from the microwave and carefully spooned it into the bowls. "Do you want crackers?"

"Mom, you don't have to do all this," Shaya said.

"Shaya, I am your mother and my job is to mother. Now, do you want crackers?" she asked again.

Shaya smiled. "Yes, please," she said. "Thanks, Mom."

It felt good to smile. It felt good to have her mom here. She knew she was facing a long, heart-wrenching road ahead, but for right now, in this moment, she was okay. She heard a faint phone chirp and realized it was an incoming text but had no idea where she had left her phone.

"I'll get your phone," Ben said as he stood from the table. "I put it on the nightstand for you." He returned quickly and handed the phone to Shaya.

"It's Jexi," she said. "I'm going to need to let her know something soon. She is extremely worried about me."

"Invite her over," Ben said.

"There's plenty of soup," Attie added.

Shaya took a deep breath and let it out slowly. "I don't know if I can talk to her right now. This is so hard."

Attie sat next to Shaya and took her hand. "I'm with you. I'm not leaving until you kick me out. Let Jexi come over, and I can help you share the news."

Ben placed his hand on her other arm. "Babe, you need to tell her sooner, rather than later. You know how she gets when she's worried about you. It's important to let her know you are okay . . . ish."

"Okay," Shaya said. "I hear you." She typed a message into the phone inviting Jexi to the house and pressed the send button. Within thirty seconds, the doorbell rang.

The three of them looked at each other and laughed. Shaya walked to the door and opened it. "Jexi," she said. "What a surprise! Seriously though, how did you get here so fast?"

"You invited me over, so here I am!" Jexi exclaimed.

"You were out waiting in the car, weren't you?" Shaya asked.

Jexi hung her head sheepishly, "Maybe," she whispered. She raised her head and sniffed. "I smell soup. I like soup."

Shaya moved aside. "Come in. Mom's got soup in the kitchen. There is plenty."

"Do you want crackers?" Attie asked with a grin.

Shaya giggled. She was glad that she was surrounded by some of her favorite people. It didn't ease the pain completely, but it helped to fill the hole left in her heart.

Over dinner, Jexi nudged Shaya and said, "Took you long enough to resurface. I was beginning to wonder if I needed to send a search party."

"I know," Shaya said, as tears began to flow once again. "I'm sorry I scared you. But the last two days have been difficult, and I just needed some time to process it all. You know how I get."

Jexi nodded, noticing the tears. "What's wrong?"

Ben explained again what they learned at the doctor's appointment. By the time he was done, Jexi was crying also. "Oh, Shaya," she said. "I'm so sorry! What can I do?"

Shaya looked at her. "I love that you want to help, but this time, there is nothing you can do."

"Except pray," Ben stated. "Please pray."

"Prayer is the BEST thing we can do," Attie said. "And we will do a lot of it. Remember, our God is a God of miracles!"

"Of course, I'll pray," Jexi said. "But I'm also here for you if you need anything else from me. You know that. Would distracting you help any?"

Shaya shrugged. "I'm not sure," she answered.

Jexi stood up and launched into a dance and song of "John Jacob Jingleheimer Schmidt." Shaya couldn't help but laugh through her tears.

"Jexi, you should take your show on the road. Really, I mean it," Ben said, laughing. "Or at least take it out of here!"

Jexi pretended to be hurt by his comment. "Actually, Shaya, I was going to ask if you would be up for some wedding planning?"

Shaya grinned. "Wedding planning? Now you're talking! I mean, don't get me wrong, the dance was nice and all, but planning a wedding is right up my alley! First off, what are your colors going to be?"

CHAPTER SIX

The next few months passed in a blur of chaotic wedding preparations. With Hunter and Jexi set on a fall wedding, there was plenty to do and not much time to do it. Shaya found joy in helping Jexi plan, throwing herself into color palettes, flowers, dresses, and cake tastings helped her focus on something brighter, something hopeful.

The day before the wedding, Jexi and Shaya scheduled a little girl time while Ben and Hunter were off doing their own thing. They started with a relaxing trip to the salon for manicures and pedicures, soaking in the calm before the whirlwind of the big day. Afterward, they headed to Jexi's apartment to pack her honeymoon suitcase, though it quickly turned into an impromptu fashion show. One by one, Jexi modeled her summer outfits, twirling around the room and laughing as Shaya gave thumbs-up or playful critiques.

Hunter was taking her to Aruba, the island where they had first met, turning a sweet beginning into the perfect honeymoon.

As they packed and giggled, the girls reminisced about how Jexi had met Hunter on that cruise.

"I totally knew that you had a crush on him from the start," Shaya said to Jexi. "It was so obvious to me!"

"Okay, okay, I'll admit it," Jexi confessed. She touched the purple bracelet on her arm thoughtfully. She recalled the day Hunter had given it to her on the cruise. It was intended to be a trinket prize for her beating him in the mini-golf match, but it turned out to be so much more. "I did have a bit of a crush. But I was also so very confused because I thought I was still in love with Brennan. He had just stood me up at the altar, remember? I was nowhere near able to think about a new relationship."

"I know," Shaya said. "But you know that was God's plan, right? To introduce you to your future husband."

"I can see it now, in hindsight," Jexi said. "I am amazed at how God works. He knows exactly what, and who, I need in my life. I'm still learning, I know, but the more I trust in His will rather than my own, things always work out so much better for me!"

"That is how incredible our God is," Shaya said. "It reminds me of that Scripture in Jeremiah. You remember that one, right? Jeremiah twenty-nine, verse eleven? 'For I know the plans I have for you—'"

Jexi cut her off. "Declares the Lord. 'Plans to prosper you and not to harm you, plans to give you hope and a future.'"

Shaya smiled. "You are growing, small one, I am proud."

"I have a great mentor," Jexi giggled. "But you know that verse applies to you as well. We don't need to talk about it now. But I want you to think about how God has plans for you, and they are good. He loves you just as much as He loves me."

Shaya's eyes bubbled with unspilled tears. "Has the student now become the teacher?" she asked sarcastically. "I know, I know. I won't forget, I promise." She paused. "Okay. Are you all packed? Do you have everything?"

"I think so," Jexi replied excitedly. "I can't believe I'm getting married tomorrow! For real!"

"You deserve it, Jex," Shaya said.

Jexi sighed. "I won't lie though, after what happened with Brennan, I'm a bit scared that Hunter won't show up tomorrow."

"No chance," Shaya said. "That boy is head over heels for you. There is no way he isn't coming. He knows how much Brennan hurt you and he'd never do the same. He will never leave you hanging. Besides, Ben PROMISED to make sure he gets there on time."

"Good ole Ben," Jexi said. "You have a good one, Shaya. I'm happy for you." She stopped and put her hand over her mouth. "I mean, except for, well, you know . . ." she sputtered and trailed off.

Jexi's phone rang, which was a welcome diversion. "It's Angelica!" she squealed.

"Hola!" Jexi said into the phone.

"Hola, *mi amiga,"* Angelica answered. "I want to wish you many blessings for your wedding. I pray for you always and lift you up to the Lord."

"Gracias!" Jexi said. "Thank you, Angelica! That means so much to me!"

"I wish my Juan Carlos and I can come tomorrow but we cannot. We will be praying for you all of the day. We are thanking you for the offer to bring us, but we want to be able to spend more time with you and the whole family. The baby cannot travel yet."

"Oh, Angelica, I understand," Jexi said. "It's okay! We will miss you, but we'll send you pictures!"

There was a knock on the door. "I'll get it," Shaya mouthed. She opened the door to a huge bouquet of flowers. Shaya gasped at the size of the arrangement in front of her.

From behind the flowers came a voice, "Delivery for Jexi Driscoll."

Jexi turned and stopped midsentence when she saw the flowers. "Wow!" she yelled.

"You okay?" Angelica asked.

Jexi quickly responded. "Yes, but can I call you back?"

"Es okay," Angelica replied. "We can talk in a couple of days."

Jexi hung up the phone and approached the delivery man. "What on earth is all this?" she asked.

"Duh, they are flowers," Shaya quipped.

"Got that, Sherlock," Jexi quipped back. She took the flowers and set them on the coffee table. "I don't have any cash," she said as she searched her pockets.

"Here," Shaya said as she handed the delivery boy a few dollars.

"Thanks," he said.

Shaya shut the door. "What's the card say?"

She opened the card and began reading. *"Jexi, I never thought I would find a girl like you in my entire life. And now here I am, about to marry you. You have made me the happiest man alive, and I thank God for you. I am going to spend the rest of our lives showing you just how much I love you. Love, Hunter."*

Shaya squealed. "That is so sweet!" she said.

Jexi blushed. "It is, isn't it? I'm so happy."

Shaya and Jexi spent the rest of the night talking, laughing, and goofing around with each other. Jexi thought about how God had blessed her with such an incredible best friend. She wasn't sure if she could tell Shaya how much she appreciated her. But she wanted to try.

As they drifted off to sleep, Jexi whispered, "Shay, you asleep yet?"

"No," came a soft whisper back.

"I'm about to make it weird," Jexi said.

"Oh, no, don't," Shaya groaned.

"I have to," Jexi said. "Or I'll never forgive myself."

"Okay, just keep it short," Shaya begged.

"Here goes," Jexi responded. "Shay, you're my best friend in the entire world. I share everything with you, and there is no one I'd rather have with me right now. Thank you for being my matron of honor and, more importantly, thank you for being the most awesome friend anyone could ask for." She began to choke up toward the end, so she stopped.

"Are you crying?" Shaya asked, sniffling.

"No," Jexi lied. "It's my allergies."

"Mine too," Shaya fibbed. "And you're welcome. I feel the same way." There was a short pause. "Now shut up and go to sleep. That's enough weird for the night."

CHAPTER SEVEN

The alarm was loud and woke the girls with a start. Jexi sat up and smashed the off button. "Get up, sleepyhead," she said to Shaya. "I'm getting married today!"

Shaya rubbed her face. "Alright, alright, I'm up," she said as she swung her legs over the side of the bed.

Their hair salon appointment was set for seven-thirty that morning, so the girls had to get moving quickly. Jexi's parents had parked their home-on-wheels in the alley behind her apartment, and her mother was joining them for the outing.

"Do you think Mom's up yet? Should I call her?" Jexi asked.

Shaya looked at her watch. "Yeah, I would, we have to be at the salon in fifteen minutes."

Jexi looked out the window as she opened the contact list on her phone. Before she could hit send, her mother appeared out of the RV door, looking beautifully put together. Jexi smiled. *Of course, she is on time and looking amazing*, Jexi thought.

Louise climbed the stairs to the apartment and knocked gently on the door. Jexi opened it with a smile and pulled her mother into a hug.

"Do you even need to go to the salon?" Jexi teased. "You already look done up!"

Louise laughed. "I didn't really do my hair," she said. "I'm letting the stylist work her magic today."

Jexi snorted. "You're hilarious!" she said.

Shaya walked into the living room. "Are we all ready to go?" she asked.

After their appointment, the girls headed straight to the church. The pews were simply adorned with floral arrangements in the colors

Jexi had chosen: plum, lavender, and white. Matching candles flickered softly at the front, and a three-stranded cord hung from a wooden board on the altar, symbolizing the union she and Hunter were about to enter.

Since this was technically Jexi's second time planning a wedding, she and Hunter had chosen not to worry about all the extras of a formal affair. They wanted something meaningful, not overwhelming.

In the bridal room, the ladies began to dress. Louise and Shaya chatted easily as they changed, filling the space with light conversation. Jexi slipped into her wedding gown, her thoughts drifting to Hunter. He had called that morning, his voice full of excitement as he told her how ready he was to make her his wife.

Still, a knot twisted in her stomach. As much as she wanted to believe everything was fine, part of her couldn't shake the fear, *What if he didn't show up?* She shook her head quickly, trying to silence the doubts. It was Brennan who had proven himself untrustworthy, not Hunter. Hunter would be there. She had to believe that.

She heard her mother gasp and turned to find Louise standing there, hands over her mouth, tears welling in her eyes.

"Mom . . ." Jexi began, glancing down at her dress. "This one isn't nearly as fancy as—"

Louise shook her head, cutting her off gently. "Don't even say it. For some reason, you're more beautiful today than you were then. It doesn't matter how fancy the dress is. Today, you are absolutely stunning."

Jexi blinked, feeling her own tears rising. "Really, Mom?" she whispered. "You think so?"

Louise stepped forward, brushing a tear from her cheek as she took Jexi's hands in hers. "I know so," she said softly. "Because today, you're not just wearing a dress, you're walking in peace, in love, and in God's strength. It shows in every part of you."

Jexi smiled, her lips trembling as she pulled her mom into a hug. For a moment, she let herself rest in the warmth of it, the kind of embrace that steadied her when everything else felt uncertain.

Shaya smiled. "It makes a difference when you are marrying the man God intended for you," she said.

Jexi turned back to the mirror and studied her reflection. She had to admit, there was a transformation. She might actually be glowing. Her dress was simpler than the one she'd worn before, but somehow, it felt more beautiful. The bodice had a soft V-neckline with delicate, ruffled cap sleeves, and the skirt was made of layered tulle that floated into a small chapel train. She absolutely loved it. From the moment she tried it on, she'd known it was the dress she would wear to marry Hunter.

Out of the corner of her eye, she saw Shaya standing behind her and turned around. She had trusted Shaya to choose her own matron of honor dress, and she hadn't been disappointed. Shaya looked stunning in the knee-length plum gown. The skirt was made from the same airy tulle as Jexi's, but fuller, with rhinestones clustered near the waist to give the effect of a sparkling belt. She had even matched Jexi's V-neckline and ruffled cap sleeves perfectly.

Jexi stepped forward and wrapped her arms around her best friend. "You look amazing," she said.

Shaya stepped back. "Stop. You're making it weird." The girls both broke out into laughter.

"Deal with it," Jexi quipped. "It's my wedding day."

There was a knock at the door and Louise called, "Who is it?"

"It's Gary," came the reply, and Louise went to open the door. "It's time," he said as he approached Jexi. "Ready to walk down the aisle for real? You know, since the first one was just practice?" He snickered at his own joke.

Jexi laughed. "Daaaad," she whined. Secretly, though, she appreciated her dad's humor. She looked at her mom and then her best friend. "Let's do this!"

The first notes of the bridal march began to play, and Jexi took a deep breath as she hooked her arm through her father's. Ahead of them, her brother, Mike, offered his arm to their mother and escorted her to her seat, then slipped into the pew beside her.

Shaya stepped forward next, meeting Ben at the center. The two walked down the aisle together, taking their places at the front. Jexi caught the quiet, loving glance they exchanged as they stood side by side, and it made her smile. That kind of love, the steady, deep kind, was exactly what she hoped for with Hunter.

Jexi and her father approached the entrance of the sanctuary. As the guests rose to their feet, her father looked down at her and gently patted her hand.

"I'm so happy for you, honey," he whispered.

Jexi felt tears welling, her throat tightening with emotion. She swallowed hard, willing herself to stay composed. "Thanks, Dad," she said. "I love you."

"Love you, too, kiddo," her dad replied. "Now, let's get you hitched."

This was it. The moment she would walk toward the man who had shown her what love was meant to look like.

They began walking down the aisle, and Jexi's eyes locked with Hunter's. She heaved a sigh of relief. He was there, waiting, just like he promised.

Hunter's breath caught the moment he saw her. Jexi looked breathtaking, and he couldn't stop the tears that slid down his cheeks. He was still in awe that God had chosen someone so special, so full of grace and strength, to be his wife. As she drew closer, he whispered a quiet prayer of thanks for all that God had given him.

The ceremony flowed seamlessly, every word and moment filled with meaning. When they finally kissed, the crowd erupted into cheers and applause.

The reception was held in one of the church's gathering rooms. It was simple but sweet; just cake, punch, and a few light snacks. Nothing extravagant, but Jexi wouldn't have changed a thing. She couldn't stop smiling. Everything felt perfect.

The hours passed in a joyful blur, hugs, well-wishes, and kind words from friends and family, all celebrating the beginning of their new life together.

Before long, it was time to go. Jexi and Hunter were heading to their hotel room in northwest Arkansas that evening, choosing to leave now instead of rushing out at dawn. Their flight would depart at 8 a.m., and by afternoon they'd be in Florida, ready to board their cruise ship. By evening, they'd be sailing toward Aruba, just the two of them, beginning a brand-new chapter.

CHAPTER EIGHT

The morning after Jexi's wedding, Shaya woke early. The excitement and whirlwind of the previous day had left her completely drained. She'd gone straight to bed as soon as she and Ben arrived home, and now, with the joy of the wedding behind her, she felt an urgency to get back to reality.

Before getting ready for church, she padded quietly into the office and opened her planner to check the week ahead. Her breath caught when she saw what was written on today's square. This would have been her due date. In the rush and busyness, she'd forgotten to erase it, and now the date stared back at her like a painful reminder.

Her whole body was clenched with grief, and tears spilled down her cheeks. The thought that she could be in labor right now overtook every other feeling. All she could see was how different her life might have been if things had gone the way they were supposed to.

She looked up toward the heavens and whispered, "Why, God? Why?" Her voice trembled, rising to desperate sobs, and then to wailing. "What did I do wrong? Am I being punished for something?"

Ben burst into the office, panic etched across his face. Without hesitation, he rushed to her side and pulled her into a gentle embrace. "Baby, what's wrong?" he asked, struggling to make sense of her sobs. Then his eyes landed on the date marked on the calendar, and at that moment, he understood why his wife was a crumpled mess.

"We can stay home from church," he whispered softly, trying to offer comfort.

Shaya shook her head, her voice still trembling but clearer now. "I want to stay home . . . but I feel this pull to go. I don't know why."

Ben took a step back and met her gaze. "I think you're being called to go because God wants to comfort you."

He paused, then corrected himself quietly, "Comfort *us*."

Shaya remained still, wrestling with the thought. How could God want to comfort her when He had taken away the baby? *He could have just let me have the baby if He truly wanted to comfort me,* she thought bitterly.

Finally, she looked up at Ben and gave a small shrug. "Yeah, I guess," she muttered. "I'll go get ready."

"Shaya, hold on," Ben pleaded. "I understand your skepticism, but remember what Jesus says in Matthew eleven, twenty-eight through thirty?"

Shaya stopped in her tracks. She could recite that passage by heart because she had studied it so many times.

Ben began, "Come to Me, all you who are weary and burdened, and I will give you rest."

Shaya joined in, "Take My yoke upon you and learn from Me, for I am gentle and humble in heart, and you will find rest for your souls. For My yoke is easy and My burden is light."

Not surprisingly, she felt calmer. Not happier, but calmer. She knew that this was the peace of God that she was experiencing. She silently said a prayer of thanks to Him for not abandoning her in this painful time.

The drive to church was quiet. Neither of them spoke much; words felt inadequate for what she was feeling. Instead, Ben reached over now and then to squeeze her hand or brush a stray lock of hair from her face, a silent promise that he was there.

Shaya stared out the window, watching familiar streets pass by, her mind tangled in memories and prayers. She felt the weight of loss pressing on her heart, but beneath it, a small, stubborn thread of hope, like a faint light just beyond the horizon.

When they pulled into the church parking lot, Ben glanced at her with a gentle smile. "Whatever God has planned for us," he said quietly, "we'll face it together."

Shaya nodded, swallowing the lump in her throat. Maybe, she thought, this was exactly where she needed to be.

The couple walked into the church hand in hand, greeting others as they passed by. When they reached the front of the church, Ben kissed Shaya on the cheek and released her hand. "See you soon," he said as he walked back to join the worship band.

Shaya took her usual seat where her family would soon join her. As she waited, she repeated the passage from Matthew over and over in her mind.

Shortly before the music began, her family filled in their seats and hugs were exchanged. Aunt Jessie looked at Shaya and could instantly tell that she was upset about something. Jessie whispered into Shaya's ear, "Are you okay?"

Shaya looked at Aunt Jessie. That woman was so intuitive that there would be no way she could keep this secret from her. Tears rolled down her cheeks in silence. Shaya could not speak. She leaned over and gave Jessie another hug.

"We'll talk after church, okay?" Jessie asked.

Shaya nodded.

The worship was incredible as always and Shaya found herself crying even more while praising God. She knew that no matter what, she would praise God for being who He is and for being so good to her. Even if she was a bit angry with Him right now.

Pastor Dave had a sermon that hit Shaya right in the heart. He discussed how God is our refuge and strength and that He is able to carry all of our burdens. His key passage was Matthew eleven, verses twenty-eight through thirty, the very passage Ben had shared with her that morning. Shaya knew that was no coincidence. God always showed up in the most perfect way.

Pastor Dave talked about how we live in a fallen world and that bad things happen, no matter who we are. He stressed the importance of pursuing God's will and standing on God's promises because then we will experience the comfort of God in difficult times. It was not uncommon for Shaya to cry in church, but today had her bawling more than usual. She felt that the message had been sent to her directly from God.

After church, Aunt Jessie invited Shaya to her house for a while, to talk and just be together. She suggested to Ben that he pick Shaya up there once he was finished with his duties in the worship band.

The ride to Jessie's was quiet. Shaya sat quietly beside her aunt, her thoughts still swirling, while Jessie drove with a calm, steady presence.

Once inside, Jessie busied herself in the kitchen, preparing hot tea and carefully setting out cups and saucers. The gentle clinking of dishes filled the room as Shaya settled at the kitchen table, folding her hands in her lap, unsure what to say.

Jessie sat down across from her and offered a warm, understanding smile. The silence between them wasn't uncomfortable; it was filled with unspoken care, waiting patiently for Shaya to find her words. She finally reached for Shaya's hands and took both in hers. "Kiddo, I know you better than you think I do, and I know that something is wrong," Aunt Jessie said to Shaya. "Talk to your auntie."

Shaya wept as the dam finally broke. She poured out the whole story, getting pregnant, the overwhelming joy she had felt, then the crushing blow of the miscarriage. Her voice trembled as she confessed the hardest part: learning that conceiving again would be difficult, and that even if she did get pregnant, she might never be able to carry a baby to term.

Jessie didn't speak. She simply held her, tears streaming down her own cheeks as she rocked Shaya gently in her arms. The kitchen around them faded away, the only sound the quiet sobs of shared sorrow.

After a long moment, Jessie pulled back slightly and brushed a tear from Shaya's cheek. "Shaya, I understand your pain. I truly do," she said softly. Her voice wavered as she added, "I'm going to tell you something I've never told anyone. It's a secret I've held onto for twenty-six years."

She paused, drawing in a shaky breath. Her fingers tightened slightly around her teacup. "Oh dear," she whispered, her eyes glistening. "This isn't easy to say . . . ."

Shaya dried her eyes. "Jessie?"

Jessie looked up at Shaya. "I'm just going to say it; you know, rip the Band-Aid off, right?" There was a long pause. "I got pregnant at nineteen. I wasn't married, but the boy I was with promised that he loved me. I was in college and living on my own for the first time. I thought I knew it all and believed we were going to spend our lives together. I fell victim to his lies. As soon as we found out I was pregnant, he seemed happy about the prospect of a baby. But after a few days, he changed his mind and demanded that I have an abortion." Jessie stopped and sighed. "He said that we weren't married and weren't financially stable enough to be parents. He stated that I would have to quit college and that we were just not emotionally ready. He promised that after we got married, we would be able to have more children. No one would ever know about this, and we could go on with life as normal."

Shaya's face showed a mix of shock and sadness. "So, you had the abortion? What happened?"

"Sadly, yes," Jessie confessed. "I was so under this boy's control that I couldn't see any other way to make him happy. I thought that he knew what was best for our future, despite knowing that it was wrong. I pushed everything I had learned and my feelings aside and convinced myself that I could go through with this and be okay. I hoped that God would somehow not know about it if I never shared it with anyone."

Shaya sat in silent disbelief for a moment. "So, did he marry you? I don't remember you ever being married."

Jessie shook her head slowly. "No," she said, her voice steady but quiet. "I broke up with him about a year later. The relationship was so toxic."

She stared down at her teacup, turning it gently in her hands. "I eventually found out he was cheating on me. I wasn't the only woman that he swore he loved. But more than that . . . I started to see how he had manipulated and controlled me. How he made me feel like I was the problem; like I was lucky he stayed with me." She paused and let out a tired breath. "It took everything I had, but I finally left him."

"And you never found anyone else or had more children." Shaya said quietly.

"No," Jessie answered. "I thought for a long time that God was punishing me because of the abortion and that was why I never found a husband. I dropped out of college and buried myself in God's Word. I wanted to do everything I could to get back into His good graces and get His forgiveness. Before I knew it, I was a traveling missionary."

"You never told anyone else?" Shaya asked.

"No, I couldn't bring myself to tell anyone," Jessie said. "I was too ashamed. There are no words to explain the shame and guilt I felt. I tell you what, that devil sure can use those emotions to destroy you if you let him. And I did, for a while. I finally got to a place where I was able to talk to God and ask for His forgiveness. He helped me to understand that I didn't need to carry that shame around anymore. But I still didn't want anyone else to know."

"I'm guessing that is when you figured out that you couldn't earn His forgiveness?" Shaya asked.

Jessie nodded. "I know it isn't exactly the same situation. But I lost a baby too. And was never able to have another. Unfortunately, mine was by choice, but I feel the loss, just the same. Seeing your pain brought mine back in a different way. I wanted you to know, you're not alone."

Shaya grabbed Jessie's hand. "Thank you for feeling safe enough to share that with me," she said. "I love you so much."

"I love you too, Shay," Jessie said, her eyes soft with emotion. "I guess God had me share that with you for a reason, seeing as how I've not told anyone else." She reached across the table and took Shaya's hand in hers. "I suspect you might be feeling like . . . maybe He's punishing you somehow?"

Shaya's eyes filled again as she nodded slowly, unable to speak right away. "How did you know?" she finally asked.

Jessie squeezed her hand gently. "I remember feeling that way too. After everything fell apart, I thought I must've done something to deserve it. I kept asking God why He let it all happen if He really loved me." She paused, searching Shaya's eyes. "But you know what I've come to believe over the years? That His love isn't shown by what He spares us from, it's shown by how He carries us through it." Jessie wiped the tears from her cheeks and continued. "He *is* carrying you, even if it doesn't feel like it right now. Neither of us are being punished by God. That isn't the way He works. Like the pastor said this morning, we live in a fallen world. The devil still has some control, for now. We just do the best we can and continue to worship and serve God."

Shaya reached for her aunt and pulled her into a tight embrace. Tears streamed freely down Shaya's cheeks, but this time they weren't just from pain. They were from being seen, heard, and loved.

CHAPTER NINE

Shaya numbly moved through the following week of work. There were several fall activities planned at school that kept her busy, but with Jexi out of town, she felt a little lost. She was anxious to have her best friend back. So many things had changed over the past couple of years but her friendship with Jexi remained unchanged.

After talking with Jessie, she was beginning to see her aunt in a new light and learning so much more about God's grace and love. She thought she knew all she needed about God, but it was becoming clear that there was a lot more for her to discover. She honestly thought she would be mad at God for what had happened to their baby, but she found herself being drawn closer to Him.

Ben was being incredibly supportive and putting her needs first. She had to admit that being pampered by him was comforting. But she knew he was hurting too. Maybe it was time she did something for him. Something simple, but meaningful. She would make him dinner. His favorite, country fried steak with mashed potatoes and gravy. *He'll love that,* she thought with a small smile.

She checked the time on her phone. If she left work now, she'd have just enough time to stop by the store on her way home. After jotting down a quick shopping list, she headed out. The grocery store wasn't busy, so she was able to get everything she needed and get home in record time.

As she unpacked the bags and began preparing the food, her heart gave a sudden little leap, light, fluttering, unfamiliar. It wasn't joy, not exactly, but . . . it was something close. Something like *hope.* While she worked, she noticed a soft humming filling the kitchen. She paused and glanced around, puzzled. The humming stopped. Then it hit her, *she* had been the one humming. The realization made her smile. It felt surprisingly good to do this kindness for her husband.

"Candles!" she said aloud to no one. "I need candles."

She heard the front door open, and Ben called, "Shaya? You home?"

"Yes, I am," Shaya replied as she practically floated toward him. He was setting his things down. "I took off a little earlier than usual."

Ben looked at his wife. She was smiling. He was confused but didn't complain. His nose picked up a delectable aroma. "What's going on? You've been staying late at work a lot lately. What changed? And what smells so good?"

"I know I've used work as a distraction," Shaya confessed. "But today, I was sitting in my office after everyone had gone home, and there in the silence, I felt comfort and peace for the first time since . . ." She stopped talking.

Ben wrapped his arms around her in a hug. "I'm so glad you were able to have that moment," he told her. "I've been praying for you."

Shaya looked into Ben's face. "I have to apologize for something," she said.

Ben looked confused. "For what?" he posed.

"For not taking care of you during all of this," Shaya said. "I was so focused on myself and my feelings that I forgot that you needed support too."

"Oh, sweetie, no," Ben said. "You have no reason to apologize. You are the one who had to endure the physical pain."

"I know, but you lost your child too," Shaya said. "You are hurting just as much as I am. Maybe not with physical pain, but the heartache. I just want you to know that I am here for you. I won't get lost in myself again."

Ben smiled softly. "I love you so much. We are going to get through this together."

Shaya pushed up onto her tippy toes and kissed him gently on the lips. "I know we will. But first, I have a surprise in the kitchen."

"That must be what smells heavenly," Ben said, sniffing the air. "Chicken fried steak?" he guessed.

Shaya shoved him playfully. "You guessed it," she whined. "I wanted to surprise you."

"You did!" Ben said. "I wasn't expecting you to be home, much less to have my favorite meal prepared. Is it ready? I'm starving suddenly!" He laughed.

Shaya led him into the kitchen where she had set the table. "Yes, it's ready," she said.

Ben's eyes widened. "Candles too? You have gone all out!" he stated.

"Nothing is too good for my husband," Shaya said, giggling.

They sat down to eat, the soft glow of candlelight flickering between them. Ben began telling her about his day at work, little frustrations, and small victories. She laughed, genuinely, and then shared a few lighthearted stories about the students, things kids said that made her shake her head and smile.There was an ease between them that hadn't been there for a while.

The food was good, but it was the company that truly fed her spirit. A quiet warmth settled over her, one she hadn't felt in a long time. She was enjoying herself. *She was enjoying Ben.* And for the first time in a long time, peace didn't feel out of reach. It was right here, sitting across from her, holding a fork and smiling back.

"Ben, I think I realized something today. I mean REALLY realized," she said.

Ben looked at her, midbite, and mumbled, "What's that?"

Shaya wiped gravy from her chin. "God hasn't left us," she said. "He's been here the whole time. Even when I was angry with Him, He didn't leave."

Ben swallowed the bite of food and nodded. "I understand," he said. "I have to admit that I have been fairly angry with Him as well. But you're right, He never left us. He allowed us to be angry. He's a good, good father and waits patiently for us to figure that out sometimes."

"You were angry?" Shaya asked.

"Yeah, I was," Ben said.

"But you never, I mean, you never said anything. You kept us going to church, you kept praying, you even quoted Scripture. I had no idea," Shaya mentioned.

"My role as a husband is to lead our family," Ben stated. "Even when I was in doubt, I knew I had to continue to push us on toward Jesus."

A tear rolled down Shaya's cheek. "Ben, I'm so sorry," she cried. Her hand covered his. "I never even thought . . . ."

"Hon, it's okay," Ben said. "I didn't want to put more on you than what you were already dealing with. I talked to Hunter a lot and that helped. I also talked to God. I told Him about my hurt and anger, and He listened. It hasn't been easy. But it helped me to be there for you when you needed me. I will always be there for you."

Shaya continued to cry. She felt so guilty for overlooking Ben's feelings. "Babe, I'm so sorry," she kept repeating.

Ben shook her hand. "Stop," he said. "None of this is on you. None of it. Okay?" He lifted her chin to look into her eyes. "Okay?"

Shaya nodded and sniffled. She took a napkin and blew her nose. Her nose honked when she blew it, and they both laughed. That peaceful feeling was returning to her. "Thank you, Ben," she said. "Thank you more than you know."

They cleaned up the dinner dishes together and went back to their playful banter. When they had put away the last dish, Shaya turned to Ben. "I think we should start talking about other options to have a family. I'm ready."

Ben hugged her. "I agree. But for tonight, let's just enjoy each other's company. We can go over options tomorrow. What's on TV tonight?" he asked.

They went to the couch in the living room, turned on the television, and snuggled together under a blanket watching one of their favorite shows.

Shaya sat up with a start. “Tomorrow! Jexi comes home tomorrow.”

CHAPTER TEN

Jexi and Hunter had enjoyed a glorious week in Aruba for their honeymoon. They were tan and tired by the time they got onto the airplane to return home. Jexi had worried about Shaya occasionally while they were gone, and she was anxious to see how she was doing. Shaya swore she wouldn't call her while they were gone and she had kept her promise, much to Jexi's dismay.

Jexi reminisced about the week as they flew. She hadn't realized that love like this could even exist. Hunter was amazing and she still couldn't believe that he was her husband! She would be forever grateful that Brennan was not God's will for her.

Hunter seemed to be reading her thoughts. He leaned over and whispered in her ear, "I am grateful that God brought us together." He gently kissed her cheek.

She looked at this handsome man who thought the world of her and was devoted to her. She smiled at him. "I am too," she said back. "I love how His plans for us are better than anything we can imagine."

With their feet safely back on the ground, both Hunter and Jexi powered up their phones and headed to the baggage claim, hand in hand. Within a couple of minutes, Jexi's phone rang in her pocket. She slipped it out, hoping it was Shaya. When she glanced at the display she raised her eyebrows. "Shaun? Why is Shaun calling?" she asked as she pressed the button to accept his call. "Hey, Shaun, what's up?"

"Oh, hi, Jexi. Is this a good time to talk?" Shaun asked.

"We are getting our luggage at the airport," Jexi answered. "But I have a few minutes before it comes out on the carousel. What's up?"

"Do you remember when we discussed the bookstore expanding to other locations?" Shaun asked.

"Yes!" Jexi exclaimed. "Did you find another store?"

"Well, potentially," Shaun said. "I'm hoping you can help me with that."

Jexi's brow furrowed. "Me? How can I help with that? Do you remember that I moved?" she said with a chuckle.

"Well, when I was down in Baxter Springs for your wedding, I noticed that there was a building for sale next to the diner where you work," Shaun said. He took a breath. "I made some inquiries while I was in town and was able to take a tour. It is a good size for a bookstore and reasonably priced, so I bought it!"

"That's wonderful!" Jexi exclaimed. "Are you coming down here to manage it?"

"No, I'm not. Has going to Aruba melted your brain?" Shaun joked. "I want YOU to manage it."

"AHHHHHHHH!" Jexi screamed and then looked around to notice everyone gawking at her. Even Hunter was attempting to shush her. "Sorry," she mouthed to the crowd. "Are you kidding me, Shaun?"

"No, I'm serious," he answered. "You are the new manager of the bookstore in Baxter Springs. I am going to come down again in a week or so to find a contractor to start the remodel. Once that is done, I will be back to help you get open."

"I don't know what to say. I am completely shocked," Jexi said.

"Just say yes," Shaun said. "I've already purchased the building. You can't back out. I need you."

Jexi stuttered, "Well, okay, I mean, thank you!" She paused. "Okay, talk to you soon." She hung up the phone.

Hunter looked at Jexi with questions in his eyes. "What was that all about?" he asked.

"Shaun bought the building next to the diner for a new bookstore and wants me to manage it!" she practically screamed. Others in the airport stared at her again. She lowered her voice. "He is coming down next week to start the remodel process! I am going to be in charge of the whole shebang!"

"Wait, what?" Hunter stammered. "I didn't realize you had been talking to Shaun about running a bookstore."

"I haven't," Jexi said. "That was totally out of the blue for me. I knew that he wanted to expand to a new location, but that's all. I never imagined he'd do something like this . . . especially in Baxter Springs. I am blown away."

Hunter squeezed her hand. "Wow, sweetie, that's quite an honor for you! I'm proud of you."

They gathered their luggage and made their way home. Jexi was bursting at the seams. She couldn't wait to tell Shaya all about the honeymoon and her new job! She was overtaken by a swift wave of guilt. She shouldn't be flaunting all of her good news in Shaya's face after all that she'd been through. No, her good fortune would wait. Shaya was most important right now.

Hunter and Jexi arrived at Hunter's house later than they expected. *I guess it's our house now*, Jexi thought excitedly. They unloaded the trunk and approached the door. Hunter dropped his luggage and took Jexi's suitcase from her, placing it next to his. "What are you doing?" Jexi asked him.

Hunter quietly unlocked the door and swiftly scooped her up into his arms before she could protest. "I'm carrying my wife across the threshold of our home." He kissed her on the side of her head and stepped into the house.

After getting the necessities put away, Jexi rushed to call Shaya. She wouldn't talk long, just enough to let her know they were home safely. She pressed the speed dial number for her best friend and waited.

Shaya answered on the second ring. "Hi!" Shaya shouted into the phone. "Did you make it home yet?"

"We just got here and put some things away," Jexi answered. "I missed you! Are you doing okay? Do you need me to come over?"

"Jex, I love the sentiment, but it's late," Shaya replied.

"If you need me, I'm there," Jexi said. "I'm okay, really," Shaya stated. "Ben has been amazing."

"Okay," Jexi said. "If you're sure."

"I am," Shaya noted. "Will you be at church in the morning?"

"We are planning to be," Jexi said.

"Good," Shaya responded. "I'll see you then. And then afterward, why don't you two come over to the house for lunch?"

"Hold on," Jexi said, "Lemme ask my HUSBAND." She pulled the phone away from her face and asked Hunter if he would be interested in going to Ben and Shaya's for lunch after church. He nodded in the affirmative. "My HUSBAND says yes," Jexi said back to the phone. "It's a good thing too, because we don't have any food in the house."

Shaya giggled at her friend's excitement. "It's a date then. Get some sleep. We will talk tomorrow. I'm glad you're home safely."

"Good night," Jexi said to Shaya and ended the call.

Jexi set her phone down on the nightstand and let out a slow breath. The house was quiet in that comforting way that only comes when everything feels settled, even if life itself was anything but. She glanced around the bedroom, taking in the unfamiliar details that were already beginning to feel like home. This was real. Aruba was over. The wedding was over. And somehow, life had only just begun.

Hunter wrapped an arm around her from behind, resting his chin on her shoulder. "You okay?" he asked softly.

She nodded, leaning back into him. "Just thinking. A lot has happened in a very short amount of time."

He smiled against her hair. "That seems to be the theme lately."

Jexi laughed quietly. "I keep waiting for it to feel overwhelming, but instead it just feels . . . right. Even the scary parts."

"That's God," Hunter said simply. "He doesn't always make things easy, but He does make them good."

She turned in his arms and looked up at him, her heart full. "I'm glad I get to do all of this with you."

"Me too," he replied, brushing a strand of hair from her face. "Every bit of it."

As they climbed into bed, Jexi said a silent prayer—of gratitude for the man beside her, of excitement for the unexpected doors opening before her, and of peace for Shaya, who was still walking through her own storm. Tomorrow would come soon enough with its conversations and decisions. For now, it was enough to rest in the certainty that God was still writing the story.

CHAPTER ELEVEN

Aunt Jessie and the rest of the family were happy to see Jexi and Hunter at church and there were lots of questions about their honeymoon. Before anyone could leave for lunch at Ben and Shaya's house, Jessie called them together with a promise of big news from Honduras.

Sitting in the sanctuary, the small group grew quiet as Jessie began. "There's a young high school girl in Honduras who needs our help," she said. "Her name is Selena, and she's in her senior year. She wants to pursue a nursing career, but there aren't any good nursing schools in Honduras." Jessie paused, then continued. "Selena's from a neighboring village near Aldea Gracia. She's also been seeing a boy her parents don't approve of. They're worried he'll lead her down a dangerous path. There are even rumors he's involved with a local gang."

She let the weight of her words sink in. "Her parents want her to come to the U.S. for school. Of course, there are a lot of wrinkles to iron out before any of that can happen, but that's the tentative plan."

"Who would she stay with?" Aunt Katie asked.

"She can stay with me," Jessie offered. "At least until she finishes high school. After that, we can look into other options."

"Wow," Jexi said. "That poor girl. Does she actually *want* to come here, or is this just her parents' idea?"

Jessie nodded thoughtfully. "Honestly, I think it's a little of both. She does want to be a nurse, and she knows the States offer the best chance for that. But she's upset about leaving her boyfriend. We'll just have to help her through that, right?"

"Oh, young love," Attie chuckled. "I remember those days."

"Should we restrict her contact with him when she gets here?" Shaya asked.

Jessie grinned. "Sounds like we're making plans already. Is that what I'm hearing?"

"Was there ever any doubt?" Katie replied with a laugh. "We need another girl in this family."

Everyone laughed and nodded in agreement.

"I'll call her parents this afternoon," Jessie said. "And Shaya, about restricting her contact with the boyfriend. I think that's something we should pray about."

Jexi hesitated, unsure if now was the time to share her own news. But the thought of Selena stepping into her shoes at the diner gave her the nudge she needed.

"Uh, guys," Jexi began. "I've got some good news, too."

Shaya jumped up, eyes wide. "You're pregnant?!"

Jexi threw up her hands. "No way! We've only been married a week!" she screeched. "Nothing like that!"

Shaya secretly exhaled in relief. She wasn't ready to handle Jexi being pregnant, not just yet.

Jexi continued, "It's nothing that big. My old boss, Shaun, called. He bought the building next to the diner. He's opening another bookstore and he wants *me* to manage it!"

Aunt Katie gasped. "No way! I saw the for-sale sign was gone, but I had no idea something was in the works!"

"He didn't want to announce it until the deal was final," Jexi said. "But can you believe it? *Manager!*"

Shaya pulled her into a hug. "You deserve every amazing gift God is giving you."

"Quit making it weird," Jexi teased, laughing as she stepped away. She turned to Katie. "Anyway, Aunt Katie, maybe Selena can take my place at the diner! She could use some income, and I'm sure she could manage a few hours a week . . . if her host mom approves." She shot Jessie a playful smirk.

Jessie looked over at Katie. "That *is* a great idea. Build her work ethic."

Katie nodded, thoughtful. "Yes, I think that would be good for her. She can start once you leave, Jexi. I'm on board!"

Smiles and chatter filled the sanctuary as the family departed for lunch. Jexi and Hunter followed Ben and Shaya to their house, and the girls eagerly slipped into familiar rhythm while preparing the meal.

While slicing carrots, Jexi looked over at her friend. "Shaya, you seem lighter than before. I'm really glad to see that."

Shaya smiled. "I am. Some. God's been helping me heal. It's not all better. I still cry. It's still hard seeing someone with a baby. But Ben and I have had moments where we've laughed. And it feels . . . nice. I wasn't sure I'd ever smile again. But God . . . you know? We're even talking about alternative options for having a family."

"That's incredible," Jexi said. "I'm proud of you."

"It's not me," Shaya replied. "It's God. I couldn't do any of this without Him. Philippians, chapter four, verse thirteen— 'I can do all things through Christ who strengthens me.' I'm leaning hard on His strength. I still don't understand how this can be His will, but I feel deep down that something good is going to come out of all of this."

Jexi was quiet for a moment, unsure how to respond. Her own faith was still so new, and she often looked to Shaya for spiritual guidance. But now, it was her turn to encourage.

"He *will* make something good come from all of it," she said. "There's that verse in Romans. I can't remember the exact reference, but it says all things work together for good."

"Romans, chapter eight, verse twenty-eight," Shaya said, already pulling out her phone. She tapped the Bible app and read aloud: "*And we know that all things work together for good to those who love God, to those who are called according to His purpose.*"

"Yes! That one," Jexi said. "I like that verse."

"I'm glad you mentioned it," Shaya said. "I hadn't thought about that one recently."

Jexi reached out and took her friend's hand. "You once told me that God's ways are always better. His will is the *only* way . . . or something like that."

"I was right," Shaya said softly. "And now you are too. Thank you for that reminder."

"And whatever happens," Jexi added, lifting her hand and hooking her pinkie, "I'm right here with you. Every step of the way. Pinkie swear."

Shaya grinned and looped her pinkie with hers. "Pinkie swear right back at ya."

They stood for a long moment in quiet understanding, until they both pulled away.

"Quit making it weird," they said in unison, then burst into laughter.

Dinner was quieter than usual, but it wasn't uncomfortable. The four of them sat around the table, passing dishes and settling into a slower rhythm. Sunlight streamed through the kitchen window, warming the room and softening the edges of the day.

"So," Ben said, breaking the silence, "one week of marriage. Any regrets yet?"

Hunter smirked. "Only that I didn't marry her sooner."

Jexi rolled her eyes but couldn't hide her smile. "Careful. I'll make you regret saying that later."

Shaya laughed softly, the sound still new enough to feel fragile but genuine. "I like this version of you two. It suits you."

Jexi glanced at her friend. "I like this version of you, too."

That earned her a small, knowing smile.

As they ate, the conversation drifted back to Selena. Shaya pushed a piece of chicken around her plate, thoughtful. "Do you think she's scared?"

Jessie's words echoed in Jexi's mind. Leaving her boyfriend, leaving everything she knows. "Yeah," she said. "I think I would be."

Ben nodded. "But sometimes scared doesn't mean wrong. It just means big."

Shaya looked at him, eyes shining. "You're getting really good at that."

He shrugged. "I live with you. It rubs off."

They finished their meal in companionable quiet, the kind that didn't demand filling. As Shaya stood to clear the plates, Jexi followed her into the kitchen.

"You really okay?" Jexi asked gently, keeping her voice low.

Shaya rinsed a dish before answering. "I'm not fixed. I don't think I ever will be completely." She paused, then added, "But I'm learning how to breathe again. Some days, that feels like a miracle."

Jexi leaned against the counter. "It is."

Shaya turned, meeting her gaze. "You've grown, you know. You don't doubt God the way you used to."

Jexi thought about that. About how faith didn't feel like pretending anymore. "I still have questions," she admitted. "But I trust Him now. Even when I don't understand."

"That's faith," Shaya said softly.

From the dining room, Ben's laugh drifted in as Hunter teased him about burning the rolls earlier. Jexi smiled at the sound. Life didn't look the way any of them had planned, but somehow, it still felt full.

Later, as Jexi and Hunter prepared to leave, Shaya hugged Jexi a little tighter than usual. "Thank you," she whispered.

"For what?"

"For staying."

Jexi pulled back just enough to look at her. "Always."

Outside, as they walked to the car, Jexi slipped her hand into Hunter's. "I think something good is coming," she said.

Hunter squeezed her hand. "Me too."

And as they drove away, Jexi felt it deep in her soul. This season wasn't about loss or fear.

It was about becoming.

CHAPTER TWELVE

The new bookstore was scheduled to open the week before Christmas; a deliberate choice Shaun had made months earlier. "There's just something about books and Christmas," he'd said. "People slow down. They want comfort. Stories matter more that time of year."

Ben and his crew had worked quickly and efficiently, transforming the once-dull building into something warm and inviting. Fresh paint brightened the walls, hardwood floors gleamed under soft lighting, and wide windows allowed natural light to pour in during the day. Hunter had been awarded the electrical contract, updating all of the wiring and installing carefully chosen fixtures that cast a cozy glow rather than harsh light.

Jexi had been swamped. There was no other word for it. Between managing the countless details involved in opening a new store and working part-time for Aunt Katie at the diner, her days blurred together. Orders had to be placed. Inventory checked and rechecked. Displays rearranged more times than she could count. Some nights, she dreamed of shelves and woke up convinced she'd forgotten something crucial.

There were shelves as far as the eye could see, stacked with as many books as one could imagine. There were classics, devotionals, children's picture books, novels with cracked spines that promised comfort, and new releases that still smelled like fresh ink. The back offered ample storage, though not nearly large enough for an event space like Shaun had in Kansas City. After much discussion, the group had decided to turn the upstairs into a coffee shop; one that could double as a small entertainment venue or be rented out for events.

Katie had generously offered to supply the coffee and a few pastries, as long as it didn't become too overwhelming for her. Jexi had promised to help however she could, though she still needed to hire someone to manage the upstairs regularly. That, she decided, would have to wait until after opening.

Outwardly, Jexi was thrilled. This was an opportunity she never imagined for herself. But privately, doubt crept in like a slow leak she couldn't quite patch.

What if Shaun had put too much trust in her?

What if she wasn't cut out for this?

The questions followed her into the night, stealing sleep and draining her energy. She lay awake replaying conversations, decisions, and "what ifs." She wanted to talk to Hunter about it, but fear held her back. He was so proud of her. He bragged about the bookstore to anyone who would listen. She didn't want to be the reason that pride dimmed.

It was two o'clock in the morning, three nights before the grand opening, when the doubts finally pushed her out of bed.

She moved carefully, easing out from beneath the covers and doing her best not to jostle Hunter. When he didn't stir, she padded quietly into the kitchen in her stocking feet and pajamas. The soft hum of the kettle felt loud in the stillness of the house.

She poured the hot water over a tea bag and carried the mug to the table, wrapping her hands around it as if warmth alone could steady her heart. Outside, the world was dark and silent. Inside, her thoughts refused to rest.

She opened the Bible app on her phone, staring at the screen without really seeing it. *What did you read when your fear didn't feel spiritual, just practical and overwhelming?*

Then she noticed the search icon.

She typed in one word: *anxiety*.

Verse after verse appeared. She scrolled slowly until one stopped her. She read it once, then again, whispering it aloud.

"*And God is able to bless you abundantly, so that in all things at all times, having all that you need, you will abound in every good work.*" "Second Corinthians, chapter nine, verse eight," she murmured.

The words felt personal. Intentional. Like God had met her right where she was sitting.

"What are you reading?" a sleepy voice asked behind her.

Jexi jumped, yelping as her phone slipped from her fingers and hit the floor. "You scared me! Why do you walk like a ninja?" she snapped, clutching her chest.

Hunter rubbed his eyes. "Sorry. I wasn't trying to scare you."

She bent to retrieve her phone, inspecting it carefully before exhaling in relief. "I was reading a Bible verse," she said.

"At this time of the morning?" Hunter asked gently. "Shouldn't you be asleep? Today's going to be busy."

Her shoulders slumped. "I haven't been sleeping well lately."

"Why not?"

She hesitated, then whispered, "I'm scared."

"Scared? Did something happen?"

"No, nothing like that," she said quickly. "I'm just worried about the store opening. What if I can't do this? Shaun's trusting me with something important. I don't want to fail."

Hunter smiled slightly. "That's what scared you?"

"It's not funny," she said defensively.

His smile faded. "I know. I wasn't laughing at you. I just thought something worse might be going on."

"Hunter, this *is* serious."

He took her hands and pulled her to her feet. "Jexi, you are one of the most capable people I know. You can't fail when God is backing you. And I know you've prayed about this."

She nodded slowly. "I have." She held up her phone. "And listen to this verse. It says He gives me everything I need to abound in every good work. I like that. It helps."

Hunter kissed her forehead. "Let's pray and go back to bed."

As they prayed, a familiar calm washed over her, stronger than before. This time, she knew exactly where it came from.

"Feel better?" Hunter asked afterward.

"I do," she said softly. "I really do."

The next morning came too quickly, but Jexi rose with a renewed sense of purpose. Before diving into the chaos of the day, she paused to thank God for the opportunity, the people around her, and the peace He'd given her in the night.

By afternoon, Shaun walked into the store and whistled. "This looks even better than I imagined! The pictures didn't do it justice."

Jexi beamed. "Thanks! But Ben's company did most of the work, Hunter redid the wiring, and Shaya's family helped decorate."

"I know," Shaun said. "But I'm impressed."

They spent hours talking about details, discounts, advertising, staffing, and events. Jexi found herself fully engaged, confident, even excited. The doubt from the night before was gone.

When Shaun finally pulled her into a side hug and said, "You did good, kid. I'm proud of you," something settled deep inside her.

As Shaun walked away to take a phone call, Jexi stood alone for a moment, looking around the store she had helped bring to life. This time, instead of fear, her heart was filled with gratitude and a quiet confidence that God would carry her through whatever came next. She had what she needed. And she was exactly where she was meant to be.

CHAPTER THIRTEEN

The opening of the bookstore was grandly successful, and the culmination would be a New Year's Eve party in the event space. Jexi would never have made it through the first few weeks without Shaun. He had stayed to help with the opening and planned to leave on New Year's Day.

Jexi sat in her office reflecting and planning for the upcoming party. Aunt Katie proved to be a Godsend, providing meals and snacks for customers and bookstore staff. She had also offered to provide food for the party. Jexi would need to hire a caterer if Katie didn't find more employees. Attie stepped in to help Katie since Jexi was swamped with the store, but she wouldn't be able to do it long-term. Jexi really hoped Selena would be a good worker.

Shaun let Jexi conduct the interviews to find clerks to work in the store, even though he sat in to supervise. She hired three new employees. Krista was a stay-at-home mom who was looking for work during the day while her children were at school. Paige was a college student in her second year, and Brian was a senior at the church school. Both students would work in the evenings and weekends, as their schedules permitted.

Selena would be arriving during the day of New Year's Eve. Jexi hoped that she would enjoy a party on her first night in the States. She didn't know how soon Selena would start working, but she knew Katie struggled to keep up with everything on her own. Perhaps the bookstore staff would consider helping Katie with the food preparations for the party and might even consider picking up hours in both places. She would talk to Katie about her ideas.

On the morning of New Year's Eve, Shaya and Jessie headed to the airport in Arkansas to pick up Selena. Both were excited to meet the young woman in person and finally get to know her better. Though they'd video-chatted beforehand, they couldn't wait to see her face-to-face.

Standing in the waiting area, holding a sign that read *"Welcome Home Selena,"* they scanned the crowd of people spilling out from the passenger boarding bridge. Finally, they spotted her, a tiny, slender girl with long, sleek black hair, nervously looking around.

When Selena noticed the sign, she started walking toward them. Jessie and Shaya waved eagerly, their faces lit up with wide grins. As Selena neared, she glanced up at the sign and then shyly up at them, offering a weak smile.

"Thank you for the sign," she said softly, her English perfect but laced with uncertainty.

"You're welcome, sweetie!" Jessie replied, wrapping her arms around Selena in a warm embrace. "Welcome to the States! We're so excited you're here!"

Selena's eyes flicked to Shaya, who was giggling beside them. Shaya could sense the tension in Selena's stiff posture, she wasn't sure how to react to this sudden, heartfelt affection from strangers.

"It's okay, Selena," Shaya said gently. "We hug a lot around here!"

The tension seemed to lift from Selena's shoulders, and she relaxed just a little. "Nice to meet you both . . . in person," she said, a real smile finally breaking through.

Jessie stepped back. "I'm sorry, honey, I didn't mean to make you uncomfortable," she said. "I am just really happy that you made it here safely and that I finally got to hug you."

"No worries," Selena said. "I am happy to see you as well. I have been nervous about coming, but I am happy to be safe in the States."

Shaya furrowed her brows. *Safe in the States?* she thought, *I wonder what she means by that?* She determined that now was not the time to ask and so she reached over to hug the young girl. "I'm happy that you're here, too!" she said. "Let's go get your luggage."

In the car on the way home, Jessie talked with Selena about all of the happenings in the town. "We have a new bookstore and there is a big party there tonight. We need to go shopping to get you a dress to wear!"

"A party in a bookstore?" Selena inquired.

Shaya laughed. "It sounds strange, but it really isn't. The bookstore has an event space upstairs. It's the perfect size for a little party."

"And New Year's Eve is the perfect opportunity for a party," Jessie added. "The bookstore is right next door to the diner where you will be working."

"I meant to tell you this before," Shaya started, "but your English is superb!"

"Thank you," Selena answered. "I have taken many years of English classes. I knew that if I wanted to be a nurse, it would be important to speak English well."

Shaya was impressed with the girl's forethought into her future. "You've wanted to be a nurse for a while then?" Shaya said.

Selena nodded. "Ever since a nurse helped to save my mother," she informed. "She was very sick. We did not know what was wrong with her other than her foot and leg were both swollen. She was getting sick and had a fever. Nothing we tried worked to get her well. A nurse who visited Aldea Gracia was told about my mother's illness, and she came to see her. We could not pay her for her services, but she insisted that she treat my mother anyway." Selena's eyes teared. "She found out that my mother had an infection from a cut on her foot. My mother did not even know that she had been cut. She gave us the medicine—antibiotics. We had mother take them for many days and she got completely better. If it had not been for that nurse . . ." Her eyes filled again and she stopped talking for a moment. "We are very grateful. And that is when I knew I wanted to help people just like that."

Shaya smiled. "That is an incredible story," she said. "You are going to help a lot of others."

Jessie interrupted, "We need to find this young lady a dress for tonight," she reminded them. "I know just the place!" She pulled off the highway in Bentonville. She drove to a little boutique and stopped the car. "Let's shop."

Selena didn't move from her spot. "But, Jessie, I don't have any money for a new dress."

"It's on me," Jessie said. "I want to do this for you. I never had a daughter of my own and now I get to borrow one for a while. Let me do this for you." She smiled sheepishly at Selena. "And for me."

Selena looked at her with wide eyes. "Really?" she asked.

Jessie's own eyes teared. "Yes, really," she said. "I feel like God is giving me this opportunity to . . . well, just giving me the chance to be a mom of sorts."

Selena grinned. "Oh, thank you, Jessie, thank you!" She jumped out of the car. "You have no idea of what this means to me!"

Jessie held her hand. "You have no idea of what this means to ME," she said quietly.

They walked into the small store and immediately began pulling dresses off the racks for Selena to try on. After they had more than they could carry, they went to the dressing room. Selena went in with the first six dresses and closed the door. After each dress, she emerged to perform a fashion show. Twenty dresses later, they had finally settled on a hot pink, knee-length, flowy dress that sparkled. It wasn't sequined but somehow had a shine that dazzled just the same. It had a V-neck with fluttery long sleeves and a silver, rhinestone belt. "This is it! I love this one!" Selena squealed. "Can I have this one?"

Shaya could see that Jessie was overjoyed. She really was looking at this as a second chance. She was happy for Jessie, but also a bit envious. Jessie looked at Shaya and instantly knew what Shaya was thinking. Jessie walked over to Shaya and wrapped her arms around her. "Just trust Him," she whispered into Shaya's ear. Jessie turned back to Selena. "If that is THE one, then we'll get it!"

Back in the car and on the way back to Baxter Springs, Selena seemed to be much more at ease with the ladies as she chattered endlessly about life in Honduras, her friends, and school. "I will miss everyone, but I am safe here." Selena paused. "Well, I mean safer than in my country."

Shaya's phone rang and she looked at the name on her screen. "Dad," she said to Jessie.

"Answer it! Don't keep Rance waiting." Jessie responded.

CHAPTER FOURTEEN

When Shaya, Jessie, and Selena got back into town, Shaya immediately drove over to her mom's house. Jessie would have to get Selena settled on her own. She had to let Attie know what was about to happen so that she wouldn't be blindsided. She had thought about calling her, but she wanted to deliver this news in person.

She pulled into the driveway and noticed a black Ram pickup truck sitting there already. *Who would be visiting Mom?* she pondered to herself. *I don't know who's truck that is, but it's probably someone from church.* She put her car into park, gathered her purse, and got out. She walked up to the door and could hear a male's voice coming from inside. She opened the door and stopped dead in her tracks. "D . . . dad?" she stammered.

"Hi, honey!" her dad greeted cheerfully as he got off of the couch to hug her.

She hugged him back. "You said you were coming to town, but I didn't know you were already here," she said questioningly.

"I was closer than I let on," Rance replied.

Shaya looked over Rance's shoulder and said, "Hey, Mom, Dad's coming to the party tonight," she said.

Her mother laughed. "I know," she said. "He just told me. It was kind of you to invite him."

Shaya was stunned. Was that a smile she saw on her mom's face? She thought her mom was furious with her father, but yet, here she is, entertaining him like he never broke their hearts. Shaya had forgiven him, but there were a couple of things she was still upset about. Wasn't her mom angry, too?

"Your mom and I were just having a soda together. Would you like to join us?" Rance asked.

Shaya gave a dramatic sigh. "I can never say no to a Pepsi." She looked at her mom. "You do have Pepsi, don't you?"

"No, of course not," Attie said. "But your dad brought some."

Shaya hugged her dad again. "I knew I could count on you!" She pulled away quickly, realizing what she had said. She turned to her mom. "Mom, is the Pepsi in the kitchen? Come with me to get one."

Attie scoffed. "You're a big girl," she quipped. "Get it yourself."

Shaya moved closer to her mother. "But I don't know what glass you want me to use," she said with some strain in her voice. "Come tell me which ones are okay."

Attie rolled her eyes. "Really? Fine. Come on." She looked at Rance. "I'll be right back. Our daughter obviously wants to talk to me in private." She followed her daughter into the kitchen. "You know what glasses we use, Shaya. What is this about?"

Shaya sighed. "What do you mean?" she spat out. "Why is he here? Why are you talking to him in such a flirty voice? And don't say you aren't. I heard the giggles."

Attie walked to Shaya and grasped both of her hands. "Forgiveness is a funny thing. It turns out that forgiving someone softens your heart and allows God's love to flow freely."

Shaya looked quizzically at her mother. "I know, I know . . . forgiveness. And I have forgiven him. Mostly. I guess I'm just confused about why you are chummy with him now."

"Well, when I decided to forgive him, I felt peace in my heart," Attie said. "I called him to let him know that I forgave him, regardless of what happens."

"You CALLED him?!" Shaya shrieked.

"Keep your voice down," Attie reprimanded. "Yes, I did. We had a lovely talk, and he apologized. As a matter of fact, we have been talking a lot lately."

Shaya's jaw fell open. "What?" she asked.

Attie smiled. “Yes,” she said. “We call each other frequently.”

Shaya didn’t know what to think or say. She stood in shocked silence for a moment. She watched as her mother got a glass from the cabinet, put a few ice cubes into it, and then filled it with the Pepsi her father had brought. When Attie handed her the glass, Shaya took it. “These are the glasses we use, dear.” Attie patted her hand and turned back into the living room.

Shaya snapped out of her confusion and commanded herself to leave the kitchen. She saw her mother and father, sitting on the couch, laughing and talking like it was old times. A thought sprang to her mind about the possibility of them getting back together. She shook off the thought, slammed the Pepsi, and headed towards the door.

“Shaya?” Attie said.

She whirled around on the heel of her foot.

“That’s my glass,” Attie said. “Please put it in the dishwasher before you leave.”

On her drive home, Shaya was still reeling from the sight she witnessed between her mom and dad. “What was that all about?” She asked out loud, almost expecting a response. But all she heard was silence.

Shaya was still in a state of shock as she dressed and prepared for Jexi’s New Year’s Eve party. Shaya expected this to be the biggest party in Baxter Springs, and they wouldn’t even be serving alcohol. She was giving herself one last appraisal when she heard the door open.

“Shay?” Ben called. “Are you about ready?”

Shaya sauntered out of the bedroom and twirled in front of her husband. “What do you think? Am I ready?”

Ben’s eyes widened. “Wow, babe, you look gorgeous!” He closed the distance between them and pulled her in for a kiss.

“Hey,” Shaya protested. “You are going to mess up my lipstick. She surveyed Ben’s appearance. “When did you get dressed for the party?”

"Oh, I took my clothes to the office with me in case I ran late," Ben explained. "Which turned out to be a brilliant plan."Across town, Jexi stood in front of the mirror, studying her reflection. Nerves jittered through her as she thought about the party that night. Despite all the planning she and Shaun had done over the past few days, making sure every detail would be perfect, doubt crept in. *What if it turned out to be a disaster?*

She shook her head, curls bouncing around her face. *Stop it*, she scolded herself. *Stop it. God is in control, as always, and worrying won't help.* She forced herself to inhale deeply, then exhale slowly through her nose. Almost immediately, she felt her nerves start to settle. She looked at her reflection one last time and said firmly, "God has seen you through every step. He won't leave you hanging now."

At that moment, Hunter peeked his head around the doorframe. "Who are you talking to?" he asked, a teasing smile on his face.

Jexi blushed, a little embarrassed. "Myself," she admitted. "Just giving myself a pep talk."

Hunter smiled, walking over to her and wrapping his arms around her. "Nervous?"

"A little," Jexi confessed. "But I reminded myself that God is in control. It helped."

"Good," Hunter said, pressing a gentle kiss to her cheek. "We should get going."

As they headed for the door, Jexi took Hunter's hand, her heart still fluttering but steady with trust. Tonight wasn't about perfection; it was about obedience, faith, and taking the next step God had placed in front of her. With one last deep breath, she squared her shoulders and walked out the door, ready for whatever the night would bring.

CHAPTER FIFTEEN

A few days after the party, Jexi and Shaya met up for their weekly girl time. They strolled through the Joplin mall, chatting and browsing the shops. Though the mall didn't have many stores left, it was still one of their favorite places to catch up.

As they stepped out of a shoe store, arms full of shopping bags, Shaya glanced over at Jexi. "Hey," she said, her tone suddenly serious. "If I tell you something, can you keep it just between us?"

Jexi scoffed and shot her a look of scorn. "Um, of course, I can. Best friend, remember?" she asked sarcastically.

"Yes, but you also have a husband that you talk to now." Shaya paused.

"I won't tell Hunter if you don't want me to," Jexi promised.

"I can't figure out what is going on with my parents," Shaya said. "It's weird. They are being all nicey-nice to each other."

Jexi laughed. "And this is a problem?" she quipped. "Why wouldn't you want them to be nice to each other?"

Shaya shook her head. "No, not just nice, but *nice,* nice, if you know what I mean," Shaya replied. "They are acting like friends. AAAANNNNNDDDD, did you see them dancing at the party? They were practically swooning. It's messing with me."

"Yeah, I saw them dancing," Jexi said. "It looked innocent enough to me." She shrugged.

"It most certainly was NOT innocent," Shaya shot back. "Mom had this look on her face that was just wrong! It was like the way she used to look at him. I think she might still be in love with him."

"Shay, what would be the harm in that?" Jexi asked. "You never wanted your parents to split in the first place. Maybe God is bringing them back together."

Shaya thought about that for a moment. "Well, I guess there isn't anything wrong with it," she conceded. "It's just cringy to watch my parents flirt so openly. Plus, they aren't telling me anything."

Jexi nodded knowingly. "Oh, I get it now. You don't want to be left out of the loop."

Shaya stopped suddenly. "You are implying that I'm nosey?" She asked.

"If the nose fits . . ." Jexi said.

Shaya shoved her playfully. "Shut up," she retorted.

Jexi giggled. "Look, your mom and dad are grown adults and have the right to live their lives without telling you everything. But, if you really must know, just ask them!"

"Can I tell you what's got me more in a tizzy than the whole flirting thing?" Shaya asked, her voice a mix of frustration and concern. "My dad's been in town for a few days, and I have no idea where he's staying. Is he at my mom's house? Because that would be highly inappropriate!"

"Then ask them!" Jexi repeated. "Seriously, if it's bugging you that much, ASK! I am sure that neither one of them is doing anything inappropriate."

"Okay, I'll ask," Shaya said.

"Good," Jexi said. "Now, come on. I want to get some cookies before we leave." She pulled Shaya in the direction of the cookie store.

"Oh," Shaya gasped. I almost forgot. "I talked to Harli yesterday."

"Really?" Jexi asked. "How is she doing? Is she still talking with Sebastian?"

"She is," Shaya responded. "She is so sad. She really likes him but doesn't see a way to have a future with him. She doesn't want to move to Honduras, and he doesn't show any signs of wanting to leave."

"That's a bummer," Jexi said. "I'll pray for them. They are so cute together!"

"She mentioned coming for a visit soon," Shaya continued. "She is working on a difficult case right now, but once it is settled, she wants to take a few days to regroup and get her head on straight."

"That will be so fun!" Jexi squealed. "Let me know when so I can make sure the bookstore is covered. I want to be free to hang out with her while she's here."

"Of course," Shaya said with a smile. "She'll want to see you too."

The girls made their way to the cookie shop for dessert, laughter trailing behind them. But as they walked, Shaya's thoughts drifted. She was still trying to make sense of her parents. *Jexi was right. Maybe it would be a good thing if they got back together. Still, it didn't add up. Why had they divorced in the first place? They never talked about it, and she had stopped asking a long time ago. Maybe it was time to ask again.*

She considered calling her brothers, Dane and Ronan. Having them home might make the conversation easier or, at least, give her some backup. But then she shook her head, trying to brush the thought away. *I'm being ridiculous,* she told herself. *I can handle this.*

Hunter and Ben met for coffee while the girls were out shopping. After placing their orders, they settled at a wobbly table in the corner.

"I've been staying in touch with Detective Sanchez from Honduras," Hunter said, leaning back in his chair. "He's thinking about moving to the States. Apparently, he's been talking with Harli and wants to see if something real could happen between them. Problem is, she's not into long-distance."

He gave a dramatic eye roll. "I swear, I'll never understand women. Anyway, I told him we'd keep an eye out for job openings here. But he wants to keep things quiet for now; so, no telling the wives yet."

Ben smirked. "I get it. Shaya had the same issue with long-distance. Harli's a great gal, though. He'd be smart to make the move. So, he's looking for something in law enforcement?"

Before Hunter could answer, the barista called out, "Hunter?"

"That's me," he said, jumping up to grab his coffee.

As soon as he returned, Ben's name was called. He headed up to the counter and came back with his drink, sliding into his seat as they picked up where they left off.

"Yeah," Hunter said, nodding. "Something police-related for sure."

Ben leaned forward slightly. "I might have an idea."

Hunter raised an eyebrow. "Yeah?"

"You hear anything about the scandal in the Joplin PD?"

Hunter shook his head. "No, what happened?"

"Couple of detectives got caught up in a corruption mess. Pretty bad, from what I heard. They cleaned house, now there are a bunch of openings," Ben said, pulling out his phone. "Let me see if I can find the article."

Hunter took another sip of his coffee, nodding. "That would be perfect for Sanchez."

"Yeah, here it is," Ben said, showing Hunter his phone.

"Oh," Hunter said after reading the news feature. "What a mess!"

"I know, right?" Ben answered. "Look, there is a link at the bottom for people to apply. We can send it to Sanchez."

"Text him now," Hunter said. "Got his info?"

"Yup," Ben nodded. "On it."

Ben's phone dinged a minute after he sent the article to Sanchez. He looked and said, "He's thrilled. He said he's going to apply right away."

"Cool," Hunter said, standing up. "I'm going for a refill."

As he pushed his chair back, his knee knocked the edge of the wobbly table. Ben's half-full cup tipped and sloshed, sending the rest of his coffee across the table.

"Ah, crud! Sorry!" Hunter grimaced, grabbing a few napkins from the nearby dispenser.

Ben chuckled as he started mopping up the mess. "You're a menace to caffeine everywhere. Looks like I need a refill too."

"It's the table," Hunter stated.

Ben shot Hunter an amused look. "The table. Right," he said.

CHAPTER SIXTEEN

Selena jolted awake and rushed to the bathroom. She had been feeling sick for the past few days and hoped she didn't have COVID. She would need to research the symptoms, but she felt like maybe nausea was one on the list. *Jessie would probably know*, she thought. *I'll ask her over breakfast.* Unfortunately, just thinking about food made her stomach churn again.

A moment later, Aunt Jessie's voice rang out from the kitchen. "Selena! Breakfast is ready!"

Dragging herself to the kitchen, Selena shuffled toward the table, looking pale and rumpled. Jessie gave her a once-over, brow furrowed.

"Lord have mercy, child, what happened to you? You look like you wrestled a tornado in your sleep."

Selena shook her head slowly. "I don't feel great," she mumbled, sliding into her chair.

Jessie's eyes narrowed. "Not feeling well?"

"Yeah," Selena said. "I think I might have COVID. Isn't an upset stomach one of the symptoms?"

Jessie paused, considering. "It *can* be," she said. "But have you been around anyone who's had it lately?"

Selena shrugged. "I'm not sure. Between school and my shifts at the diner . . . it's possible. I just feel wiped out."

"Well, eat your breakfast," Jessie suggested. "A good meal will help that nausea."

Selena clutched her mouth and ran back into the bathroom. After flushing the stool, wiping her mouth, and rebrushing her teeth, she went to the kitchen again. "I don't feel very hungry, but thank you," she said.

"I'm going to make you a doctor's appointment," Jessie said. "You really don't look well at all. Let me also call the school and tell them you won't be in today. Are you scheduled to work at the diner this afternoon?"

Selena nodded. "I'll call Aunt Katie and let her know I won't be able to cover my shift. Then I think I'll just lie down until the doctor's appointment. Thanks, Aunt Jessie." She walked back to her bedroom and shut the door.

Jessie called the school first and then dialed Dr. Daniel's office.

That afternoon, she drove a masked Selena to the clinic. Selena sat slumped in the passenger seat, her head leaning against the window. In the waiting room, she barely spoke, this time resting her head back against the wall until a nurse finally called her name.

Inside the exam room, Dr. Daniel greeted them with his usual calm demeanor. He was in his seventies now, gentle but sharp-eyed, and still wore his stethoscope like it was part of his uniform.

Selena explained her symptoms while he listened patiently, occasionally jotting notes onto a clipboard.

"Well," he said at last, "I'm going to order a few tests, just to rule things out. You're not running a fever, which is a good sign, but we'll still test for COVID, among other things. I want to get a full picture." He offered a reassuring smile. "The nurse will be in shortly to draw some blood. In the meantime, just rest here and try to relax."

As promised, a few minutes later the nurse entered, wheeling a small tray of supplies. Selena stiffened slightly at the sight of the needle. "Don't worry," the nurse said kindly, noticing her unease. "We'll make this quick."

As she prepped Selena's arm, she started chatting casually. "You know, I just moved to the States not long ago myself. Came from South Africa. Still getting used to everything here."

Selena managed a faint smile, grateful for the distraction as the nurse continued talking about adjusting to American coffee, the surprise of Midwest winters, and how friendly most of the patients had been so far.

Before Selena realized it, the blood draw was over.

"All done," the nurse said, applying a bandage to her arm. "You were great."

"Thanks," Selena murmured, sinking back into the chair.

When the nurse finished, she instructed Selena to stay put and that the doctor would return with results from most of the tests. "Would you like for me to bring Jessie back, so you don't have to wait alone?" the nurse asked.

"Yes, thank you," Selena answered.

It didn't take Jessie long to appear in her room. "Don't worry, dear girl, Dr. Daniel is extremely competent. He will get you on the road to recovery in no time," Jessie assured her.

Selena and Jessie talked about the diner, her schedule, and school for a while, and then there was a knock at the door. "Come in," Selena called.

Dr. Daniel walked into the room and shut the door behind him. He had a big smile on his face. "Selena," he began, "Good news! You don't have COVID! As a matter of fact, you aren't sick at all!"

Selena's face clouded with confusion. "Not sick?" she asked. "Then why do I feel this way? I am sick."

The doctor chuckled. "I guess I should say, you aren't contagious. I'm sure you do feel a little nauseous and worn down. My dear, you are simply pregnant! Congratulations!"

Selena stared at him in disbelief for a long moment. She was speechless, although a million thoughts were flying through her head.

Jessie spoke first. "Pregnant?" she asked in surprise. "That's an option we never considered. Right, Selena?"

Selena shook her head slowly, disbelief settling in. That particular thought had never even crossed her mind. But as she sat there in the small exam room, her memory drifted to the boy she had been dating before she came to the States. Her eyes filled with tears. "No," she whispered. "It never crossed my mind. I can't be pregnant. This is awful. This is going to ruin my life."

Jessie stood without hesitation and walked over to her. She gently took Selena's trembling hand, kneeling slightly so their eyes met. "It's going to be okay," she said softly. "We'll figure this out together."

Selena didn't answer. Her mouth opened like she might speak, but no words came. She looked utterly overwhelmed, caught between denial and the weight of reality.

Dr. Daniel cleared his throat and continued uncomfortably. "We'll need to conduct a physical exam right now, just to make sure everything is progressing normally. I'll go get my nurse and be right back." He gave a brief, sympathetic nod, then left quickly, giving them space.

Jessie stood there for a moment, unsure whether to speak or simply stay with her. Selena's shoulders shook as she cried, her face buried in her hands.

Quietly, Jessie sat beside her and wrapped an arm around her, holding her close. She didn't say anything more; words wouldn't fix this. But she stayed, offering the one thing Selena needed most right then: presence.

"I didn't expect this," Selena said softly, her voice barely above a whisper. "I am embarrassed that this is happening. I don't want you to think poorly of me." Her words broke off as another wave of emotion overtook her, and she began to cry harder.

Jessie tightened her arm around Selena, her tone calm and steady. "Sweetheart, we don't have to talk about any of this right now. And you don't need to be embarrassed. We'll let the doctor do what he needs to do, and we'll talk more at home. When you're ready."

She paused, brushing a strand of hair gently from Selena's face. "Would you like me to stay with you during the exam, or would you rather I wait outside?"

"You can go out to the waiting room," Selena murmured.

"Okay," Jessie said. "I'll be right out there if you need me." She turned and left.

Selena didn't move. She continued to cry until the doctor returned with his nurse.

Once the exam was over, Dr. Daniel washed his hands and sat down across from Selena, his expression calm and professional. "It appears you're about eight weeks along," he said gently. "And from what I can tell, everything looks fine."

Selena stared at the floor for a moment before blurting out, "It's not fine."

The doctor blinked, slightly caught off guard. "Oh . . . I'm sorry to hear that," he said carefully. "I take it this wasn't expected."

"No," she said, her voice firm now. "I'm not happy about this. I have big plans for college and my future career. A baby changes everything. I can't have this baby, Doctor. What are my options?"

Dr. Daniel nodded slowly, his tone steady. "I understand. I can refer you to the women's clinic in town. They have counselors and doctors there who can walk you through your choices, everything from parenting support to adoption, and yes, termination if that's what you decide. They'll give you the information you need without pressure."

Selena gave a small nod, her eyes distant. She was trying to be strong, but the weight of the moment was pressing hard on her.

Dr. Daniel handed Selena a folded brochure, its cover showing a soft, smiling image of a nurse and the title *Women's Health Clinic*. He offered a quick, polite smile as he gathered his notes. "You're welcome to get dressed and head home, Selena. It was nice meeting you," he said, already halfway to the door. "Be sure to schedule a follow-up at the front desk, about a month from now."

And then he was gone, the door clicking shut behind him.

Selena stared down at the brochure in her hands. The clinic's phone number was printed neatly at the bottom. She didn't open it. Instead, she set it aside on the chair beside her and slowly began to get dressed, her limbs feeling heavy, mechanical.

I'll call them as soon as we get back to Jessie's, she thought. *I have to.*

When she stepped out into the hallway, her head hung low. Her heart thudded in her chest, but it wasn't from nerves. It was shame, fear. She couldn't bring herself to meet Jessie's eyes.

How could she explain this?

Jessie had opened her home, welcomed her like family. But she hadn't signed up for this. Selena felt a knot forming in her throat. *She's going to be so disappointed. She'll put me on a plane back to Honduras before I can even explain.*

She braced herself as she approached the waiting area, uncertain of what Jessie would say, or worse, *what she wouldn't.*

"Hey, sweetheart," Jessie said gently. "You okay?"

Selena nodded but didn't look up or speak.

Jessie walked over and pulled Selena into a tight embrace. She waited a moment before speaking again. "I know it's been a hard day," she said softly. "Do you need to schedule another appointment?"

"Yes, Dr. Daniel wants me to come back in a month," Selena answered. She pulled away and walked to the counter to schedule the appointment. In her heart, she was almost sure she wouldn't need it.

The car ride home was silent. Selena stared out the window, arms folded tightly across her chest. Jessie gripped the steering wheel, glancing at her from time to time but saying nothing. She didn't want to push. Selena needed space to process, Jessie knew that much. She understood how Selena felt, and she wanted the girl to know that she would be there for her every step of the way. But right now, being quiet was the best way to show she cared.

Back at the house, Selena headed straight to her room. She picked up the phone from the wall cradle as she passed by and then shut her door with a soft click.

Sitting on the edge of her bed, she stared at the brochure for a long moment before dialing the number at the bottom. Her fingers trembled slightly as she pressed the digits, then tapped the *one* to schedule an appointment.

The line clicked, then a nasal voice came through. "Women's Clinic, how may I help you?"

Selena froze. Her throat felt dry, her heart racing. She opened her mouth, but nothing came out.

"Hello?" the woman repeated, a little sharper this time.

"Um . . . yes, hello," Selena finally managed. Her voice was thin, almost broken. "I need to make an appointment. I'm . . . I'm pregnant. And I don't want to be."

There was a pause.

"Okay," the voice replied more evenly. "When would you like to come in?"

"As soon as possible," Selena whispered through a rush of tears.

CHAPTER SEVENTEEN

Shaya walked through the front doors of the church beside Ben, smiling as she greeted familiar faces along the way. The buzz of conversation and the rich scent of coffee welcomed them into the church's coffee house, a cozy gathering spot just off the main foyer.

She got in line at the counter and, when it was her turn, ordered two Mocha Frappuccinos—no whipped cream, just the way they both liked them. Drinks in hand, she made her way back to their table, where Hunter and Jexi were already seated and chatting.

Shaya settled in next to Ben and joined the conversation, laughing softly as they caught up. The moment was light and easy, until something in her peripheral vision pulled her attention to the entrance.

She turned and froze.

Her mother had just walked in. And right beside her . . . was her father.

Shaya's jaw dropped. The hand holding her Frappuccino wobbled, nearly spilling it across the table.

Ben noticed immediately. He leaned toward her; concern etched across his face.

"Baby," he said softly, "what's wrong?"

All Shaya could do was point in the direction of her parents being welcomed. Ben turned to see what was upsetting her and then turned back. "What?" he asked. "It's just your folks."

"But they're together," Shaya whispered. "Like, together, together."

"You don't know that they are together," Ben stated. "Maybe they just got here at the same time. Besides, I saw them dancing at the party. This isn't a big deal, is it?"

Jexi raised her eyebrows and stood quickly. "Hunter needs to get on stage to lead worship. We'll see you both later."

Shaya waved at Jexi and then looked at her husband with disdain. "No big deal?!" she asked. "Didn't you see the way they were dancing at the party?"

Ben's face twisted in confusion. "First of all, they are adults. They can do what they want. But, besides that, wouldn't it be cool if they reunited?"

Shaya's disdain turned to disgust. "You can't be serious," she scoffed. "He left us. Deserted us. Remember?"

Ben nodded. "Yes, I remember. But I also remember that both you and your mom have forgiven him. What would be so bad about them rekindling their romance?"

Shaya couldn't believe her ears. "Because she's going to get hurt again," she spat out.

Ben raised his eyebrows knowingly. "So that's it," he said. "You are trying to protect her."

Shaya covered her face with her hands and sat quietly for a moment. When she lifted her eyes back to Ben they were wet with tears. She whispered, "You weren't there to see the pain she suffered. He wrecked her and she never fully recovered."

Ben said nothing but wrapped his arms around her and squeezed. Shaya regathered herself and tore herself from Ben's embrace. "It's time for service," she said softly. She stood, picked up her coffee, and walked toward the sanctuary doors.

Ben grabbed her hand to stop her. He pulled her close and murmured into her ear. "Everyone deserves a second chance at love." He kissed her on the forehead and released her.

Immediately, Shaya felt foolish. As much as she didn't want to admit it, she knew Ben was right. They were the perfect example of second chances at love. She realized that her mother should have that chance as well.

"I hate it when you're right," Shaya said to him. She took his hand. "Now let's go to church."

During the sermon, Shaya's attention drifted. From where she sat, she could see Rance seated beside her mother. At one point, he casually slipped his arm around Attie's shoulders.

Shaya's heart tensed. Part of her wanted to cheer. Her mom deserved love and happiness. But another part screamed for caution. Her mother was strong, yes. Resilient. But Shaya knew the pain Rance had caused before, and she didn't want to see it happen again.

As the congregation bowed their heads for morning prayer, Shaya closed her eyes and whispered her own. *God, please protect my mom. She's so loving, and I know she'd be thrilled to have my dad back. I would too. But I'm scared he'll hurt her again. Please, help her see clearly and make the right decision. In Jesus' name, Amen.*

After the service, as people lingered and chatted, Attie and Rance approached them. Shaya straightened as they neared.

"We'd like to have you kids over for lunch," Attie said, her tone light.

Shaya blinked. "*We*?" she asked, tilting her head slightly.

Attie smiled, choosing not to respond directly. "Will you come?"

Ben stepped in smoothly, sensing the tension. "We'd be happy to join you, Attie," he said kindly. "What time?"

"Give me about fifteen minutes to get home and set the table," Attie replied.

Shaya nodded slowly, her thoughts spinning. "Okay. We'll see you soon."

As Attie and Rance walked away together, Shaya squeezed Ben's hand. His gentle thumb rubbed against hers, silently reassuring her. Whatever lunch held, they'd face it together.

Attie had put a roast with vegetables in the crockpot before leaving for church, so lunch came together quickly once they arrived home. The dining room was quiet aside from the soft clink of silverware and the occasional polite exchange:

"Could you pass the mashed potatoes?"

"Would you like another roll?"

For a while, no one said much else.

Then, Rance cleared his throat and reached across the table to take Attie's hand. The movement drew everyone's attention. "Attie and I have decided to start dating again," he announced, his voice calm but full of energy. "Or maybe I should say *resume* dating?" He turned to Attie with a grin, clearly pleased with himself.

Attie smiled warmly in return, her eyes soft.

Shaya froze midbite and choked slightly on her roll. She coughed into her napkin as Ben leaned over and gently patted her back. "You okay?" he asked, his brow furrowed with concern.

"Yeah, I'm fine," she said after catching her breath, offering a faint smile. "Just . . . surprised." She turned her eyes to her mother. "As long as you're sure," she said carefully. "I just don't want to see you get hurt again."

Attie reached for her water glass, then set it down and met Shaya's gaze. "Sweetheart, I appreciate your concern. I really do. It tells me how much you love me." She paused. "But you don't know the whole story, what really happened when your dad left."

Shaya turned her gaze to Rance. "No offense, Dad," she said, her tone sharp but not raised, "but you *did* leave. You walked out and left Mom to carry everything alone. You broke her heart. You broke *all* of ours."

The table fell quiet again.

Rance looked down, his grin fading. Attie gently squeezed his hand but didn't speak just yet. Ben placed a comforting hand on the small of Shaya's back, grounding her.

The air in the room had shifted, thicker now, heavier with everything still unsaid.

Attie cleared her throat. "That isn't entirely true," she confessed.

"What do you mean?" Shaya asked. "That's what you told me!"

"Actually, I never really said those words," Attie said. "That was your perception of what happened. I never corrected you, but I never affirmed those thoughts either. I shouldn't have let you believe that. I shouldn't have let you remain angry with your father. I should have told you the truth."

Shaya's eyes opened wide in surprise. "Then what exactly did happen?" she asked.

"Your dad was a detective for the police department, you remember that, right?" Attie inquired.

"Yeah," Shaya answered.

"Well, the FBI approached him with a very lucrative offer and a move to Montana," Attie shared. "He wanted us to go with him. It paid considerably more than his job at the time and was a big opportunity for him."

Rance picked up the story. "I begged your mother to come with me, but she didn't want to uproot all of your lives. I was selfish. I wanted the money, the fame. I should have stayed. But when I left, I never expected things to turn out like they did. I planned to get settled and then come back for my family."

Attie lowered her gaze to her hands, her fingers gently twisting the edge of her napkin. Her voice was quiet, thoughtful.

"I was stubborn, too," she said. "I didn't want you or your brothers to have to start over in a new place, with a new school, new friends. My life was here. My family was here; my sisters and brother . . . this was home."

She glanced up briefly at Shaya, then back down.

"I was angry with him for putting his career ahead of us. I didn't believe he'd come back. And the truth is . . . even if he had, I wasn't sure I could ever leave Baxter Springs."

She paused, letting the weight of her words settle.

"I filed for divorce not long after he left. It wasn't just about him leaving. It was about me choosing to stay."

For the second time that day, Shaya couldn't believe what she was hearing. "YOU filed for divorce?!" she asked incredulously.

Attie nodded. "Yes," she said. "He was quite upset about it, but I wouldn't budge."

Rance's eyes misted. "And I just gave up," he admitted.

Shaya pushed back from the table. "I need some air," she said. Ben stood up to follow her, but she held up a hand to him. "Alone," she said. She walked out the kitchen door into the backyard. She stood by the deck railing and stared at the trees she had watched grow. She recalled planting those trees with her dad. They stood tall and strong, as she felt torn apart and defeated.

Her parents' words rumbled around in her head. She had believed all these years that her father was the reason for their broken family. She had been so angry. Even felt hate for him at times. She recalled how she had yelled at God because of her father's absence. But it hadn't been all his fault. He had tried. Sure, he had made a few mistakes, but he had tried. A wave of guilt hit her like a truck. "I'm so sorry, God," she whispered.

Almost imperceptibly, she heard a whisper in return, "It's okay, My child. I forgive you."

Forgiveness. She stood straight and suddenly needed to apologize to her dad. She practically ran into the house and grabbed him from behind in a hug. With tears streaming, she coughed out, "I'm sorry, Daddy, I'm so sorry."

Rance stood up and hugged her tight. "It's okay, darlin'. I was never mad at you. You didn't know. I am sorry. I'm sorry that I gave up on you."

Attie stood next to them, and they opened their arms to pull her into the hug. "I'm sorry, too," she cried. "I am so sorry . . . to both of you."

CHAPTER EIGHTEEN

The day of Selena's appointment at the Women's Clinic had arrived. She was scheduled to be there at one o'clock.

She'd barely touched her breakfast. The decision had been made, at least in her mind. There was no way she could have a baby and still become a nurse, not with school, not with everything ahead of her. She wasn't ready. She knew that much.

But there was one problem. She didn't have a ride.

Selena sat at the kitchen table, nervously picking at her cuticles. Jessie was at the sink, washing dishes, humming softly to herself, completely unaware of the storm building just a few feet away.

Selena's stomach twisted. She didn't want to ask. *What if Jessie said no? What if she was disappointed? What if . . . she never looked at her the same again?*

She didn't have anyone else. Not here. She took a deep breath. *Now,* she told herself. *Ask while she's distracted. She might just say yes without asking too many questions.*

Selena stood and stepped cautiously toward the sink. Her voice came out softer than she expected. "Jessie . . . do you think you could give me a ride this afternoon?"

Jessie turned slightly, drying her hands with a dish towel. "Sure, honey. Where do you need to go?"

Selena hesitated, heart thudding. "Um . . . Down around Market and Main. Five fourteen Market Street, I think."

Jessie paused, her expression unreadable for a moment. Then she set down the bowl she was washing and turned off the water. She turned to face Selena. "Isn't that the address of the Women's Clinic?" she asked.

Selena's cheeks burned as she nodded.

Jessie dried her hands. "Let's go sit in the living room," Jessie said. "We need to talk."

Selena's heart sank. She didn't want to talk about it. She just wanted to get it taken care of and over with. But since Jessie was her only transportation, she had to oblige.

They walked to the couch and sat down. Jessie took Selena's hand and held it. "Is this an appointment for an abortion?" she asked gingerly with love and concern in her voice.

Once again, all Selena could do was nod. Her throat was choked with sobs.

Jessie sighed heavily. "I was worried you might think of that option," she said. "I've been meaning to talk to you about the pregnancy, but I wanted to give you time. Space to breathe. But sweetheart . . . this can't wait any longer."

Selena's heart sank. She knew what was coming, at least, she thought she did. The lecture. The guilt. The pressure to keep the baby, to be strong, to do what everyone else thought was right.

But they didn't understand. She stared at the floor, arms wrapped tightly around herself, her voice barely audible. "I've made up my mind."

"Can I ask what's led you to that decision?" Jessie asked.

Selena looked up, eyes already brimming. "I can't have this baby. My family would never recover from the shame. I wouldn't be able to finish school. I want so badly to be a nurse . . . I *need* to be a nurse. And . . ." her voice faltered, "I don't want to raise the child of someone who hurt me. I'm not ready. Not for any of it."

Jessie's expression softened, and her eyes welled with compassion. She reached across the table, placing a hand gently over Selena's. "I hear you," she said. "And I'm so sorry for all of it. You're carrying a weight no one your age should have to. I won't pretend I don't care about what happens next. But more than anything, I want you to know you're not alone. Tell me your story."

"What story?" Selena asked.

"What happened with the boyfriend?" Jessie gently prompted. "You haven't talked about him since you got here. And as far as I can tell, you haven't called him. What is his name?"

"Gonzo," Selena said quietly. "His full name is Gonzalo Torres, but everyone calls him Gonzo. He's from a village near mine."

Jessie nodded gently, letting her speak at her own pace.

"My parents never liked him," Selena continued. "They called him a *bad boy*. He did little crimes, stealing, mostly, to make money. Nothing big, but . . . enough."

"And you loved him?" Jessie asked softly.

"I thought I did," Selena said, her voice tight. "I thought he was changing. That he'd stop stealing, get a real job, make better choices." She swallowed hard. "I never thought he would . . ." Her voice faltered, the words lodged behind shame and pain.

She looked up, bracing herself, expecting judgment. But all she saw in Jessie's eyes was love. Steady. Warm. Compassionate. It gave her the strength to go on.

"I never thought he would make me do those things," she whispered.

Jessie draped an arm around Selena, holding space for the truth to unfold. "He forced you, didn't he?" she asked.

Selena's tears fell steadily now, her body shaking with the weight of the confession. "Yes," she sobbed. "Please . . . please don't tell my parents."

Jessie didn't speak, didn't move, just held her close.

"I told him I didn't want to," Selena whispered. "I said no. But he kept saying that if I loved him, I'd do what he wanted." Her voice broke. "And I just . . . I gave up."

The silence that followed was thick with grief and helplessness.

Jessie pulled back. "I'm so sorry, sweetheart," she said, her voice barely above a whisper. "None of that was your fault. You said no. What happened wasn't love, it was manipulation. And it was wrong."

The truth of Jessie's words cut deep but also freed something inside her. "I should have listened to my parents. They warned me about him . . . about that type of boy. And now this!" Selena pointed to her stomach.

"That still doesn't make it your fault," Jessie insisted. "You did nothing wrong. But yes, now there is a child to think about."

Jessie took a deep breath and exhaled slowly. "I want to share something with you," she started. "It's a story about a young girl who found herself in the same situation as you." She looked directly into Selena's eyes. "I was that young girl."

Selena blinked, surprised. "You were pregnant?"

Jessie gave a slow, solemn nod. "I was. And I did exactly what you're thinking about doing this afternoon. I believed I had no other choice; that there were no other options. I was scared, ashamed, and convinced my life was over."

Selena's mouth fell open slightly. "You did?" she whispered.

Jessie nodded again. "I did. And for a long time, I carried that secret. I never talked about it, not even with the people closest to me. But I wish I had. I wish someone had been there to remind me that I wasn't alone. That my life wasn't over. That love and support were still possible. I made a horrible mistake . . . the worst decision I have ever made," Jessie continued. "There isn't a day that goes by that I am not saddened with regret."

Jessie reached for Selena's hand again, her grip warm and steady. "I don't want that pain for you, sweetheart," she said softly. "There *are* other options. I wish someone had told me that when I was your age. That's why I'm sharing this with you now, not to pressure you, but to let you know you're not alone."

Selena stared down at their joined hands, her tears slowing.

"I know you feel trapped," Jessie continued. "But I promise you, when we turn to God, even in our darkest moments, He shows us the way. He gives us strength we don't even know we have." Jessie paused, her eyes searching Selena's face with gentle compassion. "Can we pray together?"

Selena hesitated, then gave a small, trembling nod. "Yes," she whispered.

They bowed their heads. "Abba," Jessie began, "Thank You for Your goodness. You never fail us. You are always there for us to lean on. Selena needs You now, Father. She is scared, worried, hurting, and she needs Your love and peace. Blanket her with Your calm and show her Your will for her life and this baby's life. Shine Your light on the alternatives available to her and remind her that You are with her every step of the way. In Jesus' name, Amen."

Selena sobbed as she looked at Jessie again. "Thank you," she said. "But what alternatives could I possibly have?"

Jessie startled at the doorbell ringing. "Who could that be?" she asked. "I'm not expecting anyone." She handed Selena a tissue and stood to answer the door.

Shaya stood at the entrance; her face filled with sadness. She lifted an envelope toward Jessie.

"What's this?" Jessie asked her. "Are you okay?"

"No," Shaya answered with tears falling off her chin.

"Come, come," Jessie stepped out of the way to let Shaya walk in. She pointed to the chair in the living room. "Sit, honey." Shaya obeyed her directive. "Now, tell Aunt Jessie what's wrong."

Shaya waved the envelope at Jessie. "This is the answer from our insurance company. We had submitted a request to be considered for the fertility surgery and it . . . was . . . denied." Her shoulders heaved with sobs.

"Oh, darlin'," Jessie consoled as she gathered her in a hug.

"It's hopeless," Shaya wailed. "We'll never have a baby!" She buried her face in her hands.

"Nothing is hopeless with God, sweetie," Jessie countered.

Shaya's head whipped up and she snapped, "This surgery is the only way I can carry a baby!" she yelled.

Jessie sighed. She knew that Shaya biting at her was only out of heartache and knew not to take it personally. "Oh, the number of tears being shed today," she mused. She looked upward. "Lord, help us all," she prayed.

Shaya looked up and suddenly noticed Selena in the room staring at her wide-eyed. "Oh . . . I'm sorry." she stammered. "I didn't realize . . . I've got to go." She stood up and flew out of the door and to her car.

Selena stood up and looked at Jessie. "Thank you for praying for me, Jessie," she said. "I am going to cancel my appointment for now. I do not need a ride to the clinic after all. I am going to consider what we talked about."

Jessie smiled. "Thank You, Jesus!" she hollered.

Jessie moved around the house, tidying up and dusting as she went. She balanced a full laundry basket on her hip and headed toward the washer when she noticed Selena stepping out of her bedroom.

"Hi, child!" Jessie called warmly. "Feeling any better?"

"A little," Selena replied, hesitating near the hallway. "I was hoping we could talk. I have something on my mind, an idea, actually, if that's okay."

Jessie dropped the laundry basket with a soft thud. "Of course it's okay!" she said quickly. She reached out and gently guided Selena to the living room couch.

Once they were seated, Jessie turned to her. "What's on your mind?"

Selena looked down at her hands for a moment, then back up at Jessie. "Will you tell me what's going on with Shaya? She was talking about an operation . . . something about fertility surgery?"

Jessie leaned back with a deep sigh, her expression clouding. "Shaya has a condition that makes it very difficult, maybe even impossible, for her to carry a baby to full term," she said quietly. "She had a miscarriage not long ago . . . and it's been very hard on her. Now she's found out their insurance won't cover the surgery that might give her a chance."

She closed her eyes briefly, the weight of it all settling in her voice. "She's heartbroken. She wants to be a mother so badly."

A quiet hush settled between them.

Then Selena spoke softly, yet with a certain calm conviction. "Do you think . . . Shaya would take my baby?"

Jessie's eyes flew open. "What?" she gasped, stunned. "Shaya take your baby?"

Selena nodded slowly. "While I was in my room, I prayed," she said. "I was so confused, but then it was like God gave me clarity. What if . . . since Shaya can't have children, maybe she and Ben would adopt mine?" Her voice wavered, but her eyes were steady. "I know I can't raise a baby. I'm not ready. But Ben and Shaya . . . they're good people. Loving, kind. I already know they would be amazing parents."

Jessie sat back, her heart full and eyes beginning to mist. She reached for Selena's hand again, gripping it gently. "Selena," she said, her voice trembling, "that's one of the most selfless, beautiful things I've ever heard. You are such a blessing. God *is* working in all of this." She paused, then smiled warmly. "Let's invite them over for dinner tonight."

A grin broke across Selena's face, a soft, peaceful one. For the first time in a long while, she felt like she could breathe.

CHAPTER NINETEEN

Ben and Shaya rang the doorbell at exactly five fifteen. Selena jumped, nearly dropping the pan of dinner rolls she was pulling from the oven.

Jessie chuckled from across the kitchen. "Nervous?" she asked with a playful smile.

Selena nodded. "A little," she admitted, setting the rolls gently on the cooling rack.

"Go answer the door," Jessie said warmly. "God's going to bless this evening, just you wait and see." She winked at her encouragingly.

Selena smoothed her hands over her clothes and walked to the door. When she opened it, her heart clenched. Shaya's eyes were red and puffy, and Ben stood quietly beside her, his arm resting protectively on her back. They both looked worn down, the weight of recent heartache clearly visible.

Selena swallowed hard and offered them a small, hopeful smile. She stepped aside, opening the door wide. "Please come in."

Shaya gave her a faint smile in return and walked in with Ben behind her.

As they entered the kitchen, Shaya turned to Jessie. "What's going on?" she asked, her tone weary. "You made it sound urgent. It's a school night, you know."

Jessie placed her hands gently on Shaya's shoulders and smiled. "I know, honey. And I promise to get you home on time. You act like you're an old woman," she teased with a soft chuckle. "Just trust me, okay?"

Shaya wanted to laugh along with her aunt, but the heaviness in her chest wouldn't let her. She just didn't have it in her tonight. She didn't even want to be there, but Jessie had insisted, saying it would be "worth it." Resigned, Shaya asked dully, "What can I do to help?"

"Nothing at all!" Jessie said brightly. "Sit, sit! Dinner is ready. Selena's been a huge help."

Selena gave a shy smile as she helped bring the last of the dishes to the table. Once everything was set, they all took their seats.

Jessie reached across the table, gently taking Shaya's hand in one of hers and Selena's in the other. Her heart swelled with anticipation and gratitude. Shaya and Selena completed the circle by joining hands with Ben.

Jessie bowed her head. "Heavenly Father," she began, her voice warm with emotion, "You are so incredibly amazing. You still surprise me with Your gracious gifts every day. Thank You for bringing us together tonight. Please let Your will be made clear to us. Thank You for the food and thank You for hope. In Jesus' name, Amen."

A reverent silence followed. Plates were passed around, but no one spoke right away. Finally, Ben cleared his throat. "So . . . Aunt Jessie," he said carefully, "what was it you wanted to talk to us about?"

Jessie smiled. "Can't an aunt just invite her niece and nephew over for a casual meal?"

Ben raised an eyebrow, clearly not buying it.

Jessie gave a small chuckle. "Okay, okay. Actually, it's Selena who wanted to speak with you." She glanced at the girl and gave her a reassuring nod. "But let's eat first."

Ben and Shaya exchanged puzzled glances, then shrugged and quietly filled their plates. Jessie's cooking was as comforting as always, but the heaviness in the air was impossible to ignore.

Shaya made a polite effort at conversation, asking Selena how things were going at school and at the diner. She smiled when she was supposed to and nodded at the right moments, but her thoughts were miles away. All she really wanted was to go home, crawl into bed, and grieve in silence.

When the meal was finally over, Shaya automatically helped clear the table. She stacked dishes, rinsed them, and set them aside, all on autopilot. Jessie wiped her hands on a towel and gestured toward the living room. “Let’s all sit,” she said gently. “Selena has something she wants to share.”

Once everyone was settled into their usual seats, Jessie gave Selena an encouraging nod. “Go ahead, hon.”

Selena took a deep breath and blurted, “I’m pregnant. And I—”

The words hadn’t even settled in the room when Shaya shot to her feet, her face flushing with heat. “You had us come over to hear this?” she snapped. “After everything Ben and I have been through?” Her eyes flashed with hurt and anger as she turned her glare to Jessie. “How could you blindside us like this?” She spun toward the door. “Come on, Ben. We’re leaving.”

Ben stood, hesitating only for a second before following her.

Jessie’s voice boomed loudly, “Shaya Maxine Thatcher! You come back and sit yourself down!”

Shaya turned slowly with a look of shock. “What?” she asked.

“Sit down,” Jessie ordered. “You haven’t heard everything. Do you really think I would put you through this if that was all there was? You need to hear the rest.”

Shaya paused at the door, her hand on the knob, and turned to stare at Jessie. “Why should we stay?” she asked, her voice tight.

Jessie met her gaze calmly. “I told you, there’s more to hear. I don’t boss you very often, but I’m doing it now. Just sit and listen.”

Shaya looked at Selena, whose face had gone pale with shock. Her hands trembled in her lap, and her wide eyes brimmed with confusion and fear. For the first time, Shaya realized this wasn’t some cruel announcement meant to hurt her; it was something deeply vulnerable.

With a sigh, Shaya walked back to the couch. Ben followed silently, and they both sank into their seats. Shaya managed a stiff smile.

“Congratulations,” she said, her tone still cool but no longer biting.

Selena hesitated, glancing toward Jessie for reassurance. *Had she made a mistake? Maybe this was a terrible idea. Maybe they weren't the right people after all.*

But Jessie gave her a gentle nod. "Go on, sweet girl. They need to hear it."

Selena took a shaky breath, gripped the edge of her seat, and spoke softly, her voice barely above a whisper. "Well . . . like I said, I found out I'm pregnant." She paused, took a deep breath, and pressed on. "But I'm not in a place to raise a child. I'm too young, and I haven't even started nursing school. I came here for a future, and I still want that. So . . . what I'm trying to say is . . ." Her voice faltered, and her eyes welled with tears. "Would you take my baby?"

Ben and Shaya sat frozen. Their expressions were unreadable, caught somewhere between disbelief and shock. The room felt still, thick with emotion.

After a long pause, Ben cleared his throat. "Are you asking us to adopt your baby?"

Tears slipped down Selena's cheeks as she nodded. "Yes. I was terrified when I first found out, but then Jessie told me about your situation. I prayed . . . I asked God what to do. And I felt like He gave me this answer. I want this child to have a good life. A stable, loving family. And I see that in you two. It would be an honor to have you raise this baby."

Jessie wiped her eyes quietly. "This is why I needed you here tonight," she said. "Selena's heart is so pure in this. And I believe she's right; God is in this moment. This baby would be beyond blessed to call you its parents."

Shaya suddenly burst into tears, her voice breaking as she cried out, "YES! Yes, yes! Oh my gosh, yes!"

She covered her face, overcome, while Ben reached over and placed a steady hand on her knee. He looked across the room at Selena, his voice calm and sincere. "Selena, thank you. Thank you for even considering us for something this big." He took a breath. "But we need to pray about it, seriously, and together. We'll talk and get back to you, okay?"

Shaya's head snapped toward him, eyes wide with disbelief. "What?" she gasped. "Ben, are you kidding me?" She leaned in, her voice rising. "We've been *praying* about this for over a year. This . . . *this* . . . is the answer! Of course we want this baby. We've begged God for this miracle. And now, here it is, crying and brave and beautiful in front of us."

Ben didn't answer. He looked at Jessie and Selena. "Would you please give us a moment alone?" he asked. "I think Shaya and I need to talk in private."

"Of course," Jessie said gently. "Selena, come help me put the dishes away." The two of them quietly exited to the kitchen, leaving Ben and Shaya alone in the living room.

Shaya turned on Ben the moment they were gone. Her voice was low but sharp. "Seriously? What more do we need to pray about?"

Ben exhaled and leaned forward, elbows on his knees. "Shay, I know how badly you want a child. I want one too. But we've always promised to seek God first in everything, *together.* Even in something that feels like a miracle."

Shaya stood, arms crossed tightly over her chest. "God is *literally* putting a baby in our arms, Ben. What more confirmation do you need?" Her voice cracked, and her shoulders trembled as she sank back onto the couch. "I'm just . . . terrified she'll change her mind. And if she does, we might lose our only chance."

Ben reached over and pulled her into a quiet, firm embrace. "I get it. I really do. But this is a lifelong commitment. We're not just accepting a baby, we're stepping into Selena's story, too. She won't just disappear. She'll still be in our lives . . . in the baby's life. That changes the dynamic."

Shaya nodded into his chest, her voice muffled. "You're right. It's just . . . adoption through an agency could take *years.* We may never get another chance like this."

Ben kissed her cheek. "I wish you knew how much I want to make your dreams come true. I'm not saying no. I'm just saying that we need to seek God and His will. I am ninety-five percent convinced that this is God's path for us, but I want to be completely convinced. Let's give it a couple of days of prayer."

Shaya's shoulders fell. She knew her husband was right. She knew that praying and asking God was the best and only thing to do. She leaned back out of his arms. A few tears fell down her cheeks as she acquiesced. "You're right. I just want this so badly. I agree to give it at least one full day."

"I said a couple of days," Ben said with a chuckle in his voice.

"And I agreed to one," Shaya countered.

"A day and a half?" Ben asked with a boyish grin.

"One," Shaya stood her ground.

Ben brushed his lips on her forehead in a soft kiss. "I am such a sucker for you," he said. "Okay, one day."

Shaya smiled weakly at him and took his hand. "Let's go talk to Aunt Jessie and Selena," she said.

CHAPTER TWENTY

Hunter had just finished briefing an employee about a new assignment starting the next day when his phone rang. He glanced at the caller ID and saw that it read *Sebastian Sanchez.* He quickly answered the call. "Hey, Sanchez! Good to hear from you! How's it going?"

"It's going great, man!" Sebastian replied. "I've had a phone interview with the Joplin Police Department, and they want to have me come for a face-to-face interview as soon as I can get travel arrangements made."

"That's great news!" Hunter said. "It'd be nice having you nearby again. Solving cases together was fun."

"It was great having you help me," Sebastian admitted, chuckling. "But I must make sure I'm going by the book when I'm working in the States. As for the interview, Agent Clark has me scheduled for Friday, so I'd like to fly in on Thursday. Is there a place for me to stay while I'm there?"

"Of course, brother!" Hunter boomed. "Jexi and I have a guest bedroom that's all yours. And don't worry, I didn't let her decorate it all frilly and stuff."

Sebastian snickered. "Thanks, I appreciate it. You haven't mentioned any of this to Harli, have you?"

"Nope, not a word," Hunter answered. "We haven't even told the girls on the chance they might slip up and say something to Harli! Besides, I didn't realize you had applied for the job."

"I didn't apply right away because I needed to give it some thought. Once I did, everything happened quickly," Sebastian explained. I applied online and, within two days, Rance, uh Agent Clark, had called to schedule a phone interview."

Did you say Rance? Rance Clark?" Hunter clarified.

"Si!" Sebastian answered. "Do you know the name?"

"Rance Clark is not a common name," Hunter replied. "So, yes, I'm pretty sure I know him. But Rance is an FBI agent, not a police officer. Is this an FBI job?"

"No," Sebastian stated. "It is for the Joplin Police Department. Just like you said, they need detectives to replace the ones who were fired."

"Hmmm," Hunter hummed. "That's interesting."

"What is interesting? Who is this guy?" Sebastian demanded.

"You won't believe this. It's Shaya's dad," Hunter said.

"Seriously? Shaya's dad is FBI?"

"Yeah. Long story," Hunter replied. "He's been gone a long time and recently returned to reconnect with his family. I don't think anyone knows he is involved with the Joplin Police Department."

"Maybe it's a different guy," Sebastian offered.

"No, Buddy. Like I said, Rance is not a common name," Hunter stated. "It's the same guy. But you have given me a mystery to solve."

"Happy to help." Sebastian quipped with a laugh.

Hunter chuckled. "Listen, Sanchez, I have to step into a meeting," Hunter said. Call me when you get your flight booked so we know when to expect you."

"Will do!" Sebastian responded.

"Oh, hey," Hunter urged. "Is this still a secret? I'll need to let Jexi know you are coming, which means she will probably spill the tea to Harli."

Sebastian laughed. "No, it's okay to tell her. I am calling Harli next," he said. "Thanks, brother."

Hunter disconnected the call and stared at his phone long after the screen turned black.

"Rance Clark," he murmured to the empty room. "What are you up to?"

He turned the phone over in his hand, weighing his next move. Should he call Shaya? Ben? Ask Jexi what she knows?

No, that would just start rumors. *Maybe it would be best for me to ask Rance directly.*

For now, he would keep it to himself.

He clicked his phone back to life and touched Jexi's name to dial her number.

"Hi, honey," she answered cheerily.

"Hello, beautiful," he responded. "How is your day?"

"Better now that you are calling," Jexi replied in her very best flirty voice.

"I've got some good news," Hunter said. "Sanchez is coming to visit. He's interviewing for a detective position at Joplin PD. I told him he could stay with us."

"Oh, that is good news!" she answered. "When is he coming?"

"Thursday," Hunter said.

"Which Thursday?" Jexi asked with skepticism.

"This one," Hunter said.

"What?" Jexi squealed.

Hunter pulled the phone back to protect his hearing. "Is something wrong with that?" he asked.

There was a dramatic pause. Then a loud sigh. "Hunter! I have so much to do before we have company!"

"Jex," he said gently, "our house is always clean. You're an amazing housekeeper. Don't stress."

Jexi relaxed at his sweet words. "Thank you," she said sheepishly. "For a moment, I sounded like my mother. But we really do have a lot to get done."

Hunter chuckled. "I love you. Want me to grab dinner on the way home so you can focus on your . . . panic cleaning?"

"Hunter!" she yelped.

"Just kidding," he said, laughing. "But I'll still bring food."

"Deal. I'll make a list of what we need for Sebastian's stay. I'll probably run to the store after work."

"I'm guessing you're going to tell Shaya," he said. "Which means Harli will know before the sun sets."

"I don't tell Shaya everything," she said innocently.

"Oh, right," Hunter replied, all sarcasm.

"Well, why wouldn't I tell Shaya?" Jexi pondered. "Is this supposed to be a secret?"

"Not really," Hunter said. "But give Sebastian some time to call and tell Harli himself."

"I have a great idea!" Jexi squealed. "What if we invite Harli here too? It'd be so fun to surprise him!"

"Jexi," Hunter groaned. "Do you really think it's a good idea to get involved in their lives like that?"

"Absolutely," she said without hesitation. "Bye, babe. See you at home!"

The call ended, and once again, Hunter found himself staring at his phone.

He sighed. "Ben's gonna love this."

He scrolled to Ben's contact and hit dial, calling in backup before the madness began.Sebastian paced from his living room to his kitchen, and back again as if he were a video set on repeat. He gripped his phone tightly and felt the heat on his palm. Two thousand miles wasn't just distance. It was weight pressing on his chest. Tonight, more than ever, he felt it. He prayed Harli wouldn't think his news was foolish, or worse, desperate. With a sharp breath, he hit *call.*

After three rings, her voice came through, calm and familiar. "Hi, Sanchez, how are you doing?"

A smile tugged at his lips. "I'm good. But when are you going to start calling me Sebastian? We aren't on unofficial official business anymore."

"I don't know," Harli said, a hint of a laugh in her tone. "Habit, I guess."

Sebastian's smile faded as nerves tightened his chest. He drew in a long breath before speaking. "Well, I wanted to talk to you about something. I've got some news."

Harli's voice sharpened. "What's wrong? Do you need my help on a case?"

"No," he said with a sigh. "Nothing like that. It's . . . personal." He hesitated, then forced the words out. "I'm going to Joplin, Missouri, this Thursday. I have an interview with the Joplin PD on Friday."

There was silence. Then a gasp. "Why Joplin? Why there?"

"They fired several detectives, so there are openings." He swallowed. "And . . . I thought maybe if I were closer to you, then you might consider going on a second date with me."

Harli sat down hard on her couch, her cheeks burning even though he couldn't see her. "Oh my, Sebastian . . . that's a huge move. What about your family?"

"My brother and sister live nearby. They help care for Mama, so she won't be alone."

"But she'll miss you," Harli said softly. "And won't you miss her?"

"Of course, I'll miss her," Sebastian admitted. "But she understands I want to move to the States. And . . . there's someone I miss more than anyone right now."

Her pulse quickened. She already knew the answer but asked anyway, barely above a whisper. "Who?"

A grin colored his voice. "Hunter and Ben." He let the pause stretch just long enough before softening. "You, silly. Always you."

Harli pressed her hand to her cheek, fighting the smile that wanted to spread. His words were heavy and light all at once, like a stone thrown straight into her heart.

"I feel the same," Harli admitted. "But I still live in Texas," she reminded him. "If you go to Joplin, it will still be a long distance."

"We'll cross that bridge when we come to it," Sebastian said. "If we come to it. I might not even get the job. But one thing is for sure, a few hundred miles is a lot less than a few thousand. It's worth it for me to try." He paused and let the silence linger for a moment. "Just please say you'll consider that second date."

Harli's lips parted, but no words came right away. She twisted a strand of hair around her finger, her heartbeat loud in her ears. Finally, she whispered, "Sebastian . . . you make it hard for me to say no."

He chuckled softly, relief threading through his voice. "That sounds dangerously close to a yes."

"Maybe it's close," Harli said, her tone light but her chest tight with nerves. "But you'll have to earn it."

"I'll take *maybe,*" Sebastian replied, low and certain. "And I'll spend every mile between here and Joplin turning it into yes."

Harli closed her eyes, a smile tugging at her lips in spite of herself. The call ended with unspoken words hanging between them, half promise, half prayer.

CHAPTER TWENTY-ONE

Jexi hurriedly dialed Shaya's number, practically bouncing in her chair. She couldn't wait to share the news about Sebastian coming to town. Sure, it was a workday, and she probably should have waited until evening, but patience had never been her strong suit.

Shaya answered breathlessly on the fourth ring. "Hey, Jex, this isn't a good time. I've got a parent meeting in like thirty seconds."

"Okay, but call me back as soon as you can," Jexi said in a rush. "I've got *big* news about Sebastian Sanchez!"

Shaya sucked in a breath. "Is he okay?"

"Oh yeah, he's fine," Jexi said quickly. "Just call me ASAP, okay?"

"Alright, alright. I'll try to hurry through this meeting."

When the call ended, Jexi sat tapping her fingers against her desk, her energy too big for the quiet bookstore. She tried to distract herself with invoices and new orders but couldn't focus. She landed on a Bible study titled *Limitless Abiding,* skimmed the blurb, and laughed out loud. *"Patience, peace, and waiting on the Lord?* I think I need this one!" She had never heard of the authors but decided to order a few.

Finally, after twenty-five long minutes, her phone rang. She snatched it up before the first ring finished.

"Shaya!" she blurted. "Sebastian is coming to town this Thursday!"

"Why?" Shaya asked, her tone wary.

"He's got an interview with the Joplin PD for a detective position!" Jexi said with excitement. "You know how Harli won't do long-distance? Well, maybe this is *his* way of fixing that! Isn't it romantic? He's leaving his homeland to be with the woman he loves!"

"Slow down, turbo," Shaya laughed. "Where are you getting all this?"

Jexi huffed. "Hunter told me! Sebastian called him, he already had a phone interview, and now they want to meet him in person. He's staying with us! Hunter's even going to call Harli and tell her."

"Okay, okay," Shaya said, amusement in her voice. "But what makes you so sure this is about love and not just a big career move?"

"Come on," Jexi said. "Why else would he pick *Joplin* of all places? We both know he and Harli were sweet on each other in Honduras. And she admitted she turned him down because of the distance! This is his grand gesture!"

Shaya chuckled. "You make a good case, but Harli's in Texas, remember? That's still hours away. How's this supposed to fix that?"

"I don't know," Jexi said, smiling to herself. "But somehow, I think it will. Love always finds a way."

"Oh, you with your head in the skies," Shaya teased. "You're such a hopeless romantic. Harli's way more practical than that. I doubt a move like that would win her over."

"Oh, you with your practicality," Jexi shot back, grinning. "Maybe it's exactly the kind of move she needs to soften her heart. But I have an idea. Let's invite Harli to come up this weekend. She's been talking about visiting anyway. Why not now?"

"That's not a bad idea," Shaya admitted. "Who knows what God has in store for those two? I'll call her later, after I pray about it. But first . . . I need to talk to you about something. It's pretty serious."

Jexi's smile faded. "Are you okay?"

Shaya gave her a small, reassuring smile. "I'm fine. Really. But I do need to talk. Can we meet for lunch? It's better face-to-face."

"Of course," Jexi said immediately. "Aunt Katie's?"

"Nah," Shaya replied. "If we go there, she'll want to chat, and this isn't that kind of talk. How about the pizzeria?"

"Perfect. See you at noon."Five minutes past noon, Shaya burst through the pizzeria doors. The scent of baking dough and melted cheese hit her all at once. She spotted Jexi in a corner booth, already sipping an iced tea.

"There you are!" Jexi said, waving her hand dramatically. "I was about to send a search party!"

Shaya rushed over and slid into the seat opposite her, grabbing the other drink. "Sorry, I'm late," she said after a long swallow. "I'd make an excuse, but I don't have one."

"I'm used to it," Jexi said with a giggle. "So, what's up? You sounded so serious on the phone. Are you sure you're okay?"

Shaya nodded, though her fingers fidgeted with the straw wrapper. "I'm okay. But this is huge. Ben and I were up half the night praying. We had dinner with Aunt Jessie and Selena, and . . ." She exhaled. "I don't even know where to begin."

Jexi's eyes lit with curiosity. "Start at the *beginning,* woman! You're killing me here!"

Shaya took a steadying breath. "Yesterday, we got a letter from the insurance company, about the appeal for my infertility surgery."

Jexi's eyes widened. "Yeah? What did they say?"

"They won't cover it." Shaya's voice cracked slightly on the last word.

"Oh, Shay." Jexi frowned, shaking her head. "That's awful. What is wrong with these companies? They act like they're playing with numbers, not people."

"Yeah," Shaya murmured. "But that's not the main news I wanted to share."

Jexi blinked. "There's more?"

"Yes," Shaya said, leaning forward now. "Like I mentioned, we went to Aunt Jessie's last night. Selena was there. She's pregnant."

Jexi's jaw dropped. "What?! Selena? I didn't even know she was seeing anyone! She's barely been here three months! What about nursing school? How . . . ."

"Jex." Shaya held up a hand. "Focus."

"Right, sorry." Jexi clutched her cup like it might escape. "Go on."

Shaya's voice softened. "She doesn't want to keep the baby. She asked Ben and me to adopt it."

For a full second, Jexi just stared, her brain visibly rebooting. Then she *screamed.*

"WHAT?! Are you kidding me? Shaya, are you . . . ARE YOU SERIOUS?! Oh, my *word!*" Her voice jumped an octave as she leaned across the table. "She asked *you* to adopt her baby?! Oh, praise the Lord, this is, this is huge! This is, Shay, this could be it! The answer you've been waiting for!"

Shaya's eyes shimmered. "I know. It feels that way. But it's a lot to process."

Jexi grabbed her friend's hands, squeezing tight. "Girl, process all you want, but this is God-sized news! Selena wants you to have her baby. You and Ben! Can you even believe it? Oh, my goodness, I have chills!" She fanned herself dramatically. "Literal chills!"

Shaya laughed through her tears. "You're too much."

"And you," Jexi said, shaking her head in wonder, "are about to have the miracle you've prayed for. You are going to be a MOM!"

The waitress shot her a scowl.

Shaya looked at the waitress and mouthed the words, "I'm sorry," to her. She turned back to Jexi. "You really have to chill. They're going to kick us out!"

Jexi composed herself. "Sorry. It's just like the best news ever! I mean, this is so incredible!"

Shaya nodded. "I know, it really is. I wanted to say yes to her right away, but Ben wanted us to pray about it. And he was right; we need to seek God first and His will for us."

"Will it be awkward having Selena around? Have you thought about what happens if she wants the baby back? Will you tell the baby about her? Will she get visitation?" Jexi fired off questions so fast that Shaya barely had time to breathe.

"Jexi," Shaya said, raising her hands gently, "we've thought about all of that, and more." She sighed and leaned back against the booth.

"Ben and I have been praying nonstop for God to make things clear. We know there would need to be boundaries, real ones, for everyone's sake. It will take trust, grace, and a lot of prayer." She hesitated, her voice softening. "That's if we even say yes."

"You *have* to say yes!" Jexi blurted, eyes wide with conviction. "Oh, Shaya, think about it! This could be *your baby.* The one you've prayed for. The one you've cried over. You can't just let this pass by!"

Shaya smiled sadly, twisting her napkin in her hands. "Believe me, I've done nothing but think about it," she said. "Ben and I are going to make our decision tonight, after we pray together again. Then we'll talk to Selena."

Jexi reached across the table and took Shaya's hand, her eyes shimmering. "Let's, you and me, pray now," she said, her voice trembling with excitement.

Right there, between half-empty glasses and cooling pizza, the two women bowed their heads.

"Father," Jexi began softly, "You've heard Shaya's cries. You've seen her heartbreak and her hope. If this baby is meant to be hers, to be theirs, please make that clear to everyone involved. Give Ben and Shaya peace, give Selena courage, and wrap this whole situation in Your love. Let Your will shine brighter than any fear. We trust You with this, Lord. In Jesus' name, Amen."

When they lifted their heads, Shaya's eyes were wet with tears. "Thank you, Jex," she whispered.

Jexi grinned through her own tears. "You don't have to thank me," she said. "Just promise me one thing. If this happens, I get to be Aunt Jexi."

Shaya laughed softly. "Duh," she said sarcastically.

CHAPTER TWENTY-TWO

That day after work, Shaya rushed home, her heart light and steady with a peace she hadn't felt in months. She couldn't wait to talk with Ben and then head over to Aunt Jessie's. After all the late-night prayers and tearful conversations with God, she finally felt certain this was His plan. She had even made a neat list of questions and topics to ensure the process went as smoothly as possible for everyone.

As she pulled into the driveway, she spotted Ben's truck rolling in right behind her. She smiled to herself. *He must feel it too,* she thought.

Inside, they sank onto the couch together. Ben reached for her hands, his eyes steady and kind. "Shay," he began, "we've prayed together and separately, and I'm confident God wants us to adopt this baby. I don't have any doubts." He hesitated, smiling softly. "I do have a few things I want to talk through, but . . . ."

Shaya interrupted, grinning as she pulled a folded paper from her purse. "I made a list."

Ben laughed and shook his head. "Of course you did." He took the paper and scanned it quickly, eyes dancing with amusement. "Well, you covered everything, right down to the part about future contact. I don't have a single thing to add."

Her voice trembled. "So . . . we're doing this? Really?"

Ben's expression softened. "Yes," he said. "We're really doing this. We're going to be parents."

That word, *parents*, broke something open inside her. Tears streamed down her cheeks as she threw her arms around him. They laughed through the tears, holding on tightly, feeling the weight and wonder of what God was unfolding.

Ben leaned close, his lips brushing her hair. "Let's go talk to Selena," he whispered.

"Okay," Shaya said, pulling back with a glowing smile. "I'll call Harli on the way."

Ben raised an eyebrow. "Harli? I figured Jexi would be the first to know. You're full of surprises today."

"I already told Jexi," Shaya said with a small, knowing smile. "This is different. I'm inviting Harli up for the weekend."

Ben narrowed his eyes playfully. "Does this have anything to do with Sanchez's interview?"

Shaya's lips curved into a mischievous grin. "Maybe," she admitted. "But she's been wanting to come for a visit, and . . . now just feels like the right time."

Ben chuckled and shook his head. "You and Jexi can't help but meddle in other people's love lives, can you?"

"Shhh," she hushed him, pressing her phone to her ear. "It's ringing."

A few minutes later, she ended the call with a satisfied sigh. "She's staying with us this weekend," Shaya said absently, her mind already racing ahead.

Ben smiled. "Guess we've got some tidying up to do this week, then." He reached for her hand as they stepped out of the car. "Come on, let's go share the good news."

They held hands as they walked up the path to Jessie's front door, hearts pounding with anticipation. The porch light glowed softly against the evening sky, and for a moment, Shaya squeezed Ben's hand, half from excitement, half from nerves.

When they rang the bell, Jessie appeared almost instantly, wiping her hands on a flour-dusted apron. "Well, look at you two! Twice in one week!" she said, beaming. "What brings you to my place tonight?"

"We'd like to talk with you and Selena," Shaya replied. "If it's a good time."

"Of course, child!" Jessie said, ushering them in. "It's always a good time for family. We just finished dinner. Selena's in the kitchen baking cookies. The first batch is cooling right now. Come on in!"

As they stepped inside, the warm scent of chocolate and butter wrapped around them like a hug.

"They smell delicious," Ben said, inhaling deeply.

Jessie chuckled. "Let me fix us a plate. We've got a few minutes before the next batch comes out." She disappeared into the kitchen, then returned carrying a platter piled high with golden, gooey cookies. Selena followed behind her, also wearing an apron, her cheeks slightly pink from the heat of the oven, or maybe from nerves.

"Hi, Ben. Hi, Shaya," Selena said shyly.

"Hi, sweetheart," Shaya said with a kind smile. "We came to talk with you . . . about the baby. If you still want us to take that step with you."

Selena's eyes brightened instantly. "I do. I really do," she said, voice trembling.

Jessie encouraged everyone to sit, passing the plate of cookies around. The cozy room hummed with the quiet sound of faith and possibility.

Shaya took a deep breath. "Selena, Ben and I have prayed, hard, and we believe that God is calling us to do this. We would be *honored* to adopt your baby."

Selena covered her mouth as tears streamed down her cheeks. "Really?" she whispered.

Ben nodded gently. "Yes. Really. But we want to make sure we're all clear and comfortable before we move forward."

Shaya reached into her purse and unfolded her list, her hands trembling slightly. "We need to talk through a few things, just to protect everyone's hearts. The first is about . . . if you change your mind after the baby is born."

Selena's breath hitched.

"If we agree to this," Shaya continued softly, "we would need to know that the adoption is final. Legally, you'll have a short window where you can change your mind, but we need to be certain that the baby is truly ours. We can't go through another heartbreak, Selena. We want to be the baby's parents, fully, completely. Would you be okay with that?"

Selena wiped her cheeks and nodded slowly. "Yes," she said, voice breaking. "I love this baby, but I know I can't be a mother right now. I want you to be his or her parents."

Ben leaned forward, his tone gentle but steady. "We only bring this up because a lot of birth mothers feel differently once they hold the baby. And we understand that; it's only human. But it's something we need to talk about now, before emotions get too tangled."

Selena nodded again, tears glistening in her eyes. Jessie reached out and took her hand, giving it a reassuring squeeze.

"My dear," Jessie said softly, "this is a brave thing you're doing. And God will bless your courage. He's writing something beautiful here, even through the tears."

The room grew quiet, just the ticking of the clock and the faint aroma of another tray of cookies baking in the oven.

Selena looked at both of them, her eyes clear and steady. "I promise," she said softly. "I will not change my mind. I prayed about this, and God gave me peace about giving her, or him, to you." Her voice wavered just slightly before she added, "You were meant to be the parents of this baby."

Shaya's eyes filled with tears as she leaned forward and wrapped her arms around Selena. "You are so brave," she whispered. "We will be right here with you through it all. You're not alone in this."

Selena smiled through her tears. "I know," she said. "God reminded me of that after I talked with Aunt Jessie."

The conversation turned practical as they worked their way through the rest of Shaya's carefully written list. Each item brought a bit more peace, a bit more certainty.

When they reached the end, Ben spoke firmly but kindly. "We'll find an attorney this week and get everything in writing," he said. "We'll also take care of your medical expenses, Selena. You shouldn't have to worry about any of the costs."

Selena's eyes welled again. "Thank you. Both of you," she said. "I'm just so grateful."

Shaya smiled and asked cautiously. "Can we come with you to your doctor's appointments?"

"Of course!" Selena said, her face lighting up. "This is *your* baby. I want you there. I'll text you the date of my next appointment if I can remember it. My brain isn't exactly reliable these days."

"Pregnant brain," Jessie said.

They all laughed softly, the tension finally breaking.

Before they stood to leave, Shaya reached out and took both Selena's and Ben's hands. "Can we pray together before we go?" she asked softly.

Selena nodded, her eyes already glistening. Jessie moved closer and joined the circle, taking Selena's other hand and then Ben's.

Shaya bowed her head. "Heavenly Father," she began, her voice trembling with emotion, "we come before You tonight with hearts overflowing. Lord, You have worked in ways we could never have imagined. You've turned our waiting into hope and our hope into promise. Thank You for trusting us with this precious life growing inside Selena. Thank You for the courage You've given her and the peace You've planted in all of us tonight."

Ben squeezed her hand and continued, "Father, we ask for Your guidance in every step ahead, for wisdom, patience, and faith to walk this path with grace. Protect Selena and this baby. Keep them healthy and strong. Let Your love be the foundation of this child's story."

Jessie added quietly, "Lord, remind us that this is Your work, not ours. Help us love each other through every joy and challenge, just as You love us."

Tears streamed down Selena's cheeks. "And thank You, God," she whispered, "for giving me peace to do what's right for this baby."

There was a long moment of silence, the kind that feels sacred, before Shaya softly said, "Amen."

When they opened their eyes, there were no more words left to say. Just tears, smiles, and the unspoken understanding that God's hand was in it all. This was His will.

Ben and Shaya stepped out into the cool night air. The stars were out, glimmering above them, and for the first time in months, Shaya felt a deep, settling calm in her spirit.

"Can we go to Mom's?" she asked as they reached the car. "I want to tell her the news."

Ben smiled knowingly. "Sure. But you know she's going to go absolutely wild."

Shaya laughed. "Oh, I know. She'll lose her mind."

A few minutes later, they pulled into Attie's driveway. Shaya spotted her father's car parked by the garage and grinned. "Well, look at that. Two birds, one stone."

They walked up the porch steps hand in hand and stepped inside. Her parents were on the couch watching television.

"Hi, Mom. Hi, Dad," Shaya greeted.

Attie looked up in surprise. "Well, come on in! What are you doing out on a school night?"

"We have something to tell you," Shaya said, glancing at Ben. "And since Dad's here too, it saves us an extra stop."

Rance picked up the remote and muted the TV. "All right," he said. "What's going on?"

Shaya and Ben sat down on the love seat. They exchanged a quick look, each waiting for the other to begin.

"Well, one of you say something!" Attie urged, eyes sparkling with curiosity.

Ben cleared his throat. "You know Selena, the girl from Honduras who's staying with Jessie?"

Attie scoffed. "Of course I do. Jessie's my sister, child. Keep going."

Ben nodded, a small smile tugging at his mouth. "Well . . . what you don't know is that Selena recently told us she's pregnant."

Attie's eyes went wide, but before she could speak, Ben continued, "And . . . she's asked us to adopt her baby." He paused for dramatic effect. "We said yes."

Attie jumped off the couch like a spring uncoiling and spun in a delighted circle. "I'm gonna be a grandma!" she squealed. "Thank You, Jesus! Woo-hoo!"

Rance started clapping and laughing. "Well, how about that? Congratulations, you two!" He stood, shook Ben's hand, and pulled Shaya into a proud bear hug.

Attie was still twirling, her laughter mixing with tears as she praised the Lord. Her joy was so contagious that Shaya couldn't help laughing through her own tears. "Oh, Mom," she said, reaching for her. "I'm so happy."

The four of them stood in a tight huddle of laughter and gratitude until finally Ben glanced at the clock. "We'd better get home," he said gently.

Attie, still glowing, clapped her hands. "Then we'll celebrate this weekend!"

Shaya smiled. "We can't, actually. Harli's coming for a visit. She'll be with us Friday through Sunday. I'll tell you all about it later, but her friend, our friend from Honduras, is coming up for a job interview with the Joplin PD."

At that, Rance's smile faltered. His color drained slightly. "Who might that be?" he asked, his voice careful.

"Sebastian Sanchez," Shaya repeated. "We worked closely with him in Honduras when Juan Carlos was kidnapped. He and Harli really hit it off." She frowned. "Dad, are you okay?"

"Uh, yeah," Rance said, forcing a smile. "Sure."

Attie, oblivious to the shift, beamed. "How about Sunday dinner after church? Everyone can come!"

"I'll check with Harli and Sebastian," Shaya said. "Not sure of his travel schedule yet."

Rance cleared his throat and rubbed the back of his neck. "Before you go, I should probably tell you something."

Shaya's brow furrowed. "What's that?"

Rance looked at the floor, then over at Attie. "Well, I haven't exactly said why I'm in town, besides reconnecting with your mother and that New Year's Eve shindig." He slid an arm around Attie's shoulders. "Truth is, I came back right after Christmas to investigate the Joplin PD. There've been reports of corruption, and the FBI assigned me to the case."

Shaya's eyes widened. "You're investigating Joplin PD?"

He nodded. "Yeah. What started as a short-term assignment has stretched out. The Bureau let my partner and me stay to finish the cleanup, and, well, your mother gave me another good reason to stick around." He chuckled, but the weight of his words lingered. "We're the ones who've been letting detectives go. And we're the ones doing the interviews."

Ben blinked. "So . . . you'll be interviewing Sebastian Sanchez?"

"Friday morning," Rance said. "Small world, huh?"

Shaya stared at him, her mind spinning. "Yeah," she murmured finally. "We really do need to go. But, Dad . . ." She pointed a finger at him with a half-smile. "This conversation is *definitely* not over."

CHAPTER TWENTY-THREE

The FBI had arranged for Sebastian to pick up a rental car from the Enterprise location at the airport. As he stepped through the sliding doors into the cool Missouri air, he immediately spotted a young man holding a sign with his name on it. The clerk stood beside a white SUV, shifting his weight from foot to foot to stay warm.

Sebastian made his way over, tugging his jacket tighter, and shook the man's hand.

"I'll take us to the Enterprise store," the clerk said. "We'll check your ID, sign a little paperwork, and then the car is yours."

"Sounds great," Sebastian replied. He loaded his luggage into the back and climbed into the passenger seat, nerves humming under his skin. A new city. A new chance. And maybe . . . a certain woman.

At the rental office, Sebastian handed over his identification while the employee typed rapidly at the computer. After photocopying his documents, the young man slid a clipboard toward him.

"Just sign here. No payment needed; the charges are all taken care of."

Sebastian nodded, grateful, and signed the form. Moments later, he was walking back outside with a set of keys in hand.

He settled into the driver's seat, exhaled slowly, and plugged Hunter and Jexi's address into the GPS. When the calm voice prompted him to proceed to the nearest roadway, he shifted the SUV into drive and pulled away from the curb.Jexi was flying around the living room like a hummingbird on caffeine, dusting, straightening throw pillows that were already straight, rearranging décor items by millimeters.

"Sebastian will be here any minute!" she huffed at Hunter, who was kicked back on the couch watching TV. "Help me get this place looking decent!"

Hunter snorted, grabbed the remote, and paused his show. "Jex, the place is fine. You've been cleaning for two days. At this point, you're just moving things from one side of the room to the other. There's nothing left to clean."

"Relax?!" she shot back. "I still need to . . . well, I should . . . there's probably . . ." She stopped midrant and threw her dusting cloth at him. "Just because I *can't* think of something doesn't mean there isn't anything to do!"

Hunter grinned. "Actually, sweetheart, that's exactly what it means." He patted the couch beside him. "Come sit. Just for a minute."

Jexi glared at him, torn between indignation and the realization that he was right. The house sparkled. It smelled faintly of lemon cleaner. The throw pillows looked like they belonged in a catalog.

With a dramatic sigh, she plopped down beside him. Hunter slipped his arm around her shoulders and pressed a kiss to her temple.

"Babe," he said gently, "you are amazing and this house looks incredible. Sebastian wouldn't care anyway. He's our friend."

Jexi let herself lean into him for a moment, though her foot still bounced anxiously. "I know," she admitted. "I'm just . . . excited. And nervous."

Hunter chuckled. "Yeah, I could tell."

"I just want his first experience in the United States to be a good one," Jexi said.

Hunter brushed her lips with a kiss. "It will be," he reassured her.

They heard a car pull into the driveway. Jexi shot upright like a startled cat, grabbing her cleaning supplies. "He's here!" she squeaked and dashed to the kitchen to shove the items under the sink.

Hunter snorted, shaking his head as he pushed himself off the couch. "I'll get the door," he said, amused at her nervous frenzy.

He opened it wide. "Sebastian!" Hunter boomed. "Good to see you, friend! Come on in!"

Sebastian smiled, giving a small wave. "Hi, Hunter. Let me grab my luggage."

He retrieved his suitcase from the back of the SUV. When he returned, Hunter immediately took the bag from him, set it aside, and pulled him into a hug.

Jexi rushed into the entryway just in time. "Oh, Sebastian, it's so good to see you!" She wrapped him in a hug, squeezing a little too hard.

"Hi, Jexi!" Sebastian laughed. "Thanks again for letting me stay here."

"There is *no way* we're having you stay in a hotel," Hunter said firmly. "Come on, let's get your stuff to the guest room. Do you need to rest before we meet Ben and Shaya for dinner?"

"Nah, I'm good. I'll just change my shirt. I think I dripped butter on this one." He pointed to a faint spot, barely visible.

"I have stain remover," Jexi said instantly. "Once you change, I can treat it and toss it in the wash. Butter stains terribly!"

Hunter threw Sebastian a knowing look. "It's easier to just go along with it, man. She won't quit until she's helped."

Jexi shoved him lightly. "Not fair."

Sebastian laughed. "I've missed you both. It's really great to see you again."Later that evening, the five of them sat around a table at a popular Joplin restaurant, plates half-finished, drinks sweating on the table, and conversation bubbling nonstop.

"Ben, I really want to thank you for that job lead," Sebastian said. "I've got a good feeling about it. This might be the break I need to get to the States."

Ben nodded casually. "No problem at all. Glad to help."

Shaya's face tightened slightly. She set down her drink. "Speaking of . . ." She looked at Sebastian. "Did you know that Agent Clark is my father?"

Sebastian blinked, stunned. "No. I didn't." He paused, thinking. "Is that a good thing or a bad thing?"

Shaya let out a breath. "I don't know. I just found out about his connection myself, and I still have a ton of questions. But I do know he's in town investigating the fraud case and hiring new agents. He knows we're friends, but I'm pretty sure he'll stay impartial."

"Well, I know I can't ask him for special treatment," Sebastian said. "But I mean . . . I'd hope our friendship holds *some* influence."

"He's a good man," Shaya said, "even if I'm a little irritated with him right now. Still, he'll give you the same consideration as everyone else, I'm sure. He already knows about the great work you did in Honduras from my stories, so that might work in your favor."

"He flew you here for a face-to-face interview," Hunter added. "That has to count for something."

"I doubt he's done that for all the applicants," Jexi said with a smile. "I'm sure you'll get the job."

"Well," Ben began, "how about we take a moment to pray about your interview?"

"Yes, please," Sebastian replied. "I can always use the extra help."

The five clasped hands and bowed their heads. Ben led them in prayer, and the others joined in as they felt moved. Finally, Sebastian spoke:

"Abba, Father," he prayed softly. "You know how much I would love to have this job here in the U.S. But more than that, I want to do Your will. If it is Your will for me to have this job, then I will receive it. Thank You for Your provision and love. In Jesus' name, Amen."

When they opened their eyes, the group looked at Sebastian curiously.

"What?" he asked.

"That was a beautiful prayer," Hunter said. "I guess we never realized how deeply you felt about God."

"I understand," Sebastian said. "But after Juan Carlos was rescued, and after he convinced Andre about Jesus, I couldn't help but renew my faith. I started going to church with Manuel. You remember him, the clerk from the courthouse?" He paused. "Well, not exactly with him, but we ended up at the same church and became friends."

Shaya's eyes glistened. "I love a good coming-to-Jesus story," she whispered.

"Hallelujah!" Ben cheered. "So many blessings came out of that kidnapping. God truly worked it for His good."

"It started out so terribly," Jexi recalled, "but God had other plans."

Sebastian smiled, and a soft warmth passed over his expression. "His plans are always best. He amazes me every day. And honestly . . . another really good thing came out of that whole situation." His eyes brightened. "I got to meet Harli. I let her know I'd be here for the interview. I'm hoping she'll see this as a step toward a future with me."

Shaya giggled, unable to help herself, just as Jexi kicked her sharply under the table. Shaya jerked in surprise, glaring at her friend. "Ouch," she hissed.

Trying to recover the moment, she cleared her throat. "How about you all come over to our place tomorrow evening? Sebastian can tell us all about his interview."

"I don't want to impose," Sebastian protested. "I'm already staying with Hunter and Jexi. You shouldn't have to cook for me, too."

"I insist," Shaya said firmly, waving away the objection. "There's no reason for you to eat out. And if you don't come to our house, then Hunter and Jexi will be cooking for you anyway. So, we can do the same. I won't take no for an answer."

Sebastian raised both hands in surrender. "A home-cooked meal sounds nice. Thank you."

"Five-thirty," Ben said. "We'll see you then."

Hunter stood, tossing some cash on the table. "In the meantime, we should get back. Sebastian has a big day tomorrow."

CHAPTER TWENTY-FOUR

At five-thirty the next evening, Hunter, Jexi, and Sebastian arrived at Ben and Shaya's for dinner. After hanging up coats and exchanging hugs, they settled into the living room, conversation unfolding easily.

Shaya peeked out from the kitchen, wiping her hands on a towel. "Dinner's in the oven," she announced, "and it'll be ready in about ten minutes."

"It smells delicious," Sebastian said, inhaling deeply. "If you remember, I only get home-cooked meals when I visit my momma."

"Shaya is a fantastic cook," Ben agreed. "And tonight, she made her specialty dish, just for you."

"Oh! Speaking of." Shaya snapped her fingers. "I have something for you." She hurried around the couch and disappeared down the hall.

Sebastian frowned at Ben. "You didn't need to get me anything."

Ben raised his hands. "It wasn't me. This was all the girls. They set the whole thing up."

"Set what up?" Sebastian asked, eyebrows drawing together.

Ben, Hunter, and Jexi all lifted their eyes to look past him.

"That," Hunter said, grinning.

"It takes a lot of work to get a surprise like me here," a familiar voice chimed.

Sebastian froze. He knew that voice. Slowly, he turned, and his jaw fell open. "Harli?!" he blurted, hands flying into the air in disbelief.

"Who else?" Harli teased, her grin stretching wide. She stepped forward and wrapped her arms around him.

He hugged her tight, still stunned. "What are you doing here?"

"I came to visit the girls . . . and you," she said with a little shrug.

"They called me right after you told me about your interview. I'm between cases and had some free time, so, here I am."

Sebastian pulled her in again, his voice softening. "I am so happy to see you. There is so much I want to talk about."

Harli eased back, though her smile didn't fade. "And we will. But first, I want to hear how the interview went."

"Same!" Jexi said. "You wouldn't say a word about it on the way over here."

Sebastian laughed. "Honestly, with all the excitement, I forgot we were even supposed to talk about it." He glanced around at their eager faces. "I got the job!"

A chorus of cheers erupted.

Sebastian lifted a hand. "But wait, you won't believe this part. Remember Agent Curtis from Honduras? He called the department and put in a good word for me. Said he was impressed with my performance when we took down McGreggor. And Rance vouched for me, too."

The celebration intensified, shouts, clapping, hugs. Harli threw her arms around him again. "Congratulations, Sebastian!"

Hunter and Ben shook his hand, and Shaya and Jexi both wrapped him in warm embraces.

Suddenly, the oven timer buzzed sharply above the noise.

"Dinner!" Shaya cried, spinning toward the kitchen. Halfway there she turned back, pointing at Sebastian with delight. "And this means you're moving to the United States! That is such wonderful news!"

They followed her to the dining table, taking their seats just in time for Shaya to bring out the dishes. She carried the main entrée last. When she placed the bubbling enchilada bake in the center of the table, the entire group oohed and aahed as if rehearsed.

Sebastian clapped his hands once, leaning forward eagerly. "It looks even better than it smells!"

Shaya began serving generous portions, filling the plates with steaming enchilada bake and bright scoops of cilantro-lime rice. The aromas wrapped the table like a comforting blanket.

Sebastian took his first bite and closed his eyes. "Shaya," he said with a dramatic hand to his chest, "if the interview didn't get me to move here, this meal would have."

"Food bribery works every time," Jexi said.

Harli nudged Sebastian with her elbow. "So," she said softly, "tomorrow becomes Day One of your new life. Are you ready for that?"

He looked at her, the edges of his smile softening. "If it means being closer to you, then yes. I'm ready for anything."

Harli blinked, caught off guard, and quickly reached for her water glass, as the entire table pretended not to notice the moment.

Ben hid a smirk behind his napkin. Shaya's eyes sparkled knowingly. Jexi mouthed, *Told you so* toward Harli, who shot her a warning glance.

Sebastian cleared his throat and sat a little straighter. "I mean . . . new job, new country, new start. It's exciting."

"Sure," Hunter said, biting back a smile. "That's exactly what you meant."

The table erupted with warm laughter.

They ate, swapping stories from Honduras, reminiscing about the case that brought them all together. Harli animatedly described a few of her recent investigations, careful not to break confidentiality, while Sebastian listened with a mixture of admiration and amusement.

Toward the end of the meal, Shaya placed a warm basket of sopapillas in the middle. "Dessert," she said proudly.

Sebastian reached for one, then hesitated. "Harli, you first," he said, gesturing to the basket.

Harli arched a brow. "Chivalry . . . I like it.?" She laughed, cheeks a faint pink as she picked the smallest sopapilla. Sebastian chose the one right next to hers.

For a moment, they shared a quiet, almost private smile over the table.

It didn't go unnoticed.

And for the first time all evening, Harli didn't try to hide it.

Once the dishes had been cleared, the six of them lingered in the living room, full bellies and easy laughter making the night feel cozy.

"Let's play charades," Harli suggested, eyes bright.

Ben groaned dramatically. "Seriously? I can barely move. I overate."

Harli grinned. "Movement will help work off some calories. Come on, it'll be fun!"

"Oh, alright," Hunter agreed. "Ben, y'all don't have to go first. Jexi and I will go."

Jexi scoffed. "We will? I'm no good at this game!"

"We've got this," Hunter said, nudging her. "I think Harli's right. It'll be fun."

Jexi rolled her eyes. "Fine. But YOU'RE doing the acting."

Ben fetched the game from a closet shelf and set it on the coffee table. Hunter shuffled the cards, grabbed one, and walked to the front of the room like a performer taking the stage.

"Here we go," he said. "Get ready."

Jexi leaned forward, eyes narrowed in intense concentration.

Hunter put his hands together and opened them like a book.

"It's a book," Jexi said.

Hunter nodded, then held up five fingers.

"Five words."

He nodded again and held up two fingers.

"Second word."

Hunter placed two fingers behind each ear like little points.

"Bunny?" Jexi asked.

He shook his head. Then he pantomimed licking the back of his hand and rubbing his ear.

"Cat!" she shrieked.

Hunter grinned and held up five fingers again.

"Fifth word."

He began lifting an imaginary object onto his head.

"Getting taller? Shrinking? Growing? Downsize? Kitten?" Jexi fired off rapid guesses.

Hunter stopped, frowned, and exhaled loudly. He tried again, hands framing a round object, then lifting it toward his head.

"A plate? Plate on your head? *The Cat with a Plate!*"

Hunter stared at her, scandalized.

The room exploded in laughter.

He then mimed pinching the brim of a cap and placing it on his head.

"Hat!" Jexi screamed.

Hunter motioned for her to connect the pieces.

"The Cat in the Hat!" she blurted out just as the timer buzzed.

Hunter collapsed onto the couch in mock defeat.

Shaya wiped tears of laughter. "Seriously? How did you not get that quicker?"

"I was nervous!" Jexi pouted.

"A plate?" Hunter asked, incredulously. *"The Cat with a Plate?* Where in the world would you have read that?"

Jexi stuck her tongue out. "I was doing the best I could."

"See? Fun, right?" Harli asked.

Ben chuckled. "I can absolutely see this game tearing couples apart."

Shaya smirked. "No way! You and I can do much better. I'm up."

She picked a card and moved to the center of the room. Her clue: a song title.

Shaya raised her hand to her mouth as if singing.

"Song," Ben said. She nodded and held up three fingers.

"Three words."

She held up one finger.

"First word."

She mimed holding a phone to her ear with her thumb and pinky.

"Phone," Ben guessed.

She shook her head. He kept guessing, "Telephone . . . cell phone . . . phone call . . . ."

Shaya nodded vigorously and motioned to shorten it.

"Call?"

She beamed and held up two fingers.

"Second word."

She pointed to herself.

"Chest? Heart?"

Shaya scowled and pointed again, more emphatically.

"You?" Ben tried.

Shaya blew her breath through her lips in frustration, her glare sharp enough to win awards.

"No noises!" Harli barked. "Disqualified!"

Hunter waved her off. "Nah, let her keep going!"

Shaya pointed to herself again.

"Me?" Ben asked.

Shaya jumped up and down, triumphant.

Then she held up three fingers.

"Third word," Ben said.

She shrugged dramatically, shoulders high, palms out, eyebrows raised.

"Call me . . . call me . . ." Ben muttered repeatedly, squinting at her. "Call me . . . sometime? Call me whenever. Oh wait! It's that one song, `Call Me Maybe'!"

Shaya collapsed beside him on the love seat, laughing so hard she could barely breathe. "I thought you'd never get that! And I see what you mean. This game really *could* break up couples."

The whole group roared with laughter.

Harli laughed. "Our turn!" she announced, springing to her feet with playful determination. She spun toward Sebastian. "Come on, partner, we . . . ."

She stopped short.

Sebastian was fast asleep, head tilted back against the couch cushion, mouth slightly parted, chest rising and falling in the rhythm of someone completely gone to the world. The noise in the room hadn't touched him at all.

"Well . . . so much for our turn," Harli said, hands on her hips. "I have *no* idea how he managed to fall asleep with all that noise!"

Ben burst into laughter. "He's had a long day, Harli. A long interview, long flight, long nerves. Hard to blame the guy."

"Plus," Jexi added, "he's probably still jet-lagged. I remember that journey. It was loooooong. I slept for twelve hours straight when we got home."

Harli softened as she watched him, her smile turning tender at the edges. The boyish way his hair had fallen across his forehead made something warm tug at her chest. She reached out as if to brush it back, then stopped, catching herself, cheeks flushing.

Hunter stood and stretched. "Alright," he said, "we'll wake him up and get him home before he starts snoring." He grinned at Harli. "Don't be too hard on him. We'll make sure you two get your turn at charades tomorrow."

Harli lifted her eyebrows. "Oh, I fully intend to hold him to that."

She tried to keep the tone light, teasing, but her eyes lingered on Sebastian for a heartbeat too long, her smile a little too soft.

Jexi nudged Shaya and whispered, "She's gone."

Shaya grinned knowingly. "Completely."

Hunter stepped over and gave Sebastian's shoulder a gentle shake. "Hey, buddy," he said quietly. "Time to head out."

Sebastian stirred, blinked, and sat up straight with a confused frown. "I . . . did I fall asleep?"

The whole room erupted in laughter.

Harli crossed her arms, pretending to scold him. "Oh, you definitely did. You ditched me during charades."

Sebastian flushed and rubbed his eyes. "I'm sorry," he said sheepishly. "I . . . uh . . . didn't mean to."

Harli smiled at him, soft, genuine. "It's okay. Tomorrow, you owe me a rematch."

His tired face brightened despite the exhaustion. "Deal."

CHAPTER TWENTY-FIVE

Shaya was in an upbeat mood as she slid into the pew, ready to listen to Pastor Dave's message that Sunday morning. The sanctuary buzzed with warm conversation, sunlight pouring through the stained-glass windows in soft, colorful ribbons. She glanced down at the church bulletin on her lap and noted the title of the sermon: *"From Luck to Trust."* The focus verse printed beneath it was one she knew well—*Proverbs, chapter three, verses five and six.*

Pastor Dave stepped up to the pulpit, adjusted his glasses, and read aloud, his voice gentle but sure:

"Trust in the Lord with all your heart and lean not on your own understanding; in all your ways submit to Him, and He will make your paths straight."

Shaya let the words settle in her heart like a warm blanket. Given everything happening with the adoption, the timing of the verse felt like a personal whisper from God.

"We live in a world," Pastor Dave continued, "where people believe success comes from luck. How often do we hear, *'You got lucky!'* or *'That was a stroke of luck!'*? But as Christians, we do not rely on luck. There is no random chance in God's sovereign plan! Luck is fleeting and unreliable, Jesus is steadfast and sure."

Shaya opened her bulletin to the notes section, pen ready. She loved filling in the blanks; it helped her stay focused and soak in the message more deeply.

"Number one," Pastor Dave said slowly, giving everyone time to prepare, "is this: Luck is uncertain, but Jesus is faithful."

He paused as pens scratched across paper.

"Luck," he said, "is like the wind, unpredictable and uncontrollable. You cannot depend on it to guide your life. But Hebrews, chapter thirteen, verse eight, tells us, *'Jesus Christ is the same yesterday and today and forever.'* While luck shifts with circumstances, Jesus remains constant."

Shaya jotted the verse in the margin, her heart tightening with gratitude.

Pastor Dave continued, "Think about the storms of life, financial struggles, health issues, broken relationships . . . or even the fear of the unknown. Luck cannot anchor you in those moments. But Jesus can! He invites us in Matthew, chapter eleven, verse twenty-eight: *'Come to Me, all you who are weary and burdened, and I will give you rest.'* We don't need to flip coins in our lives; we need to bend our knees in prayer."

Shaya felt her eyes sting. With the adoption decision now set in motion, she needed this reminder. She needed the anchor. As she scribbled the Scriptures onto her page, a quiet peace settled into her spirit.

Shaya glanced toward the end of the pew where her parents sat together. Rance had his arm draped comfortably around Attie's shoulders, their heads tilted toward each other as they listened. Shaya wondered if they caught the part about broken relationships. A soft smile tugged at her lips. Their reconnection had been unexpected and, at times, downright strange for her, but she couldn't deny it: she was truly happy to see them together.

"Our second point," Pastor Dave continued, drawing the congregation's attention back to him, "is that God is sovereign over every detail. If we relied on luck, it would suggest a world without divine order, a world where God's will is nonexistent. But we know better! Our God is in control!"

A few cheers and scattered applause rose from the crowd. Pastor Dave waited, smiling warmly until the sanctuary grew quiet again.

"In Romans, chapter eight, verse twenty-eight," he said, "Paul declares, *'And we know that in all things God works for the good of those who love Him, who have been called according to His purpose.'* We can count on God working in our lives even when things seem uncertain. It wasn't luck that led Joseph from a pit to a palace; it was God's providence. It wasn't chance that parted the Red Sea for the Israelites; it was God's power."

More cheers erupted, heartfelt, energetic. Pastor Dave chuckled softly, letting the encouragement wash over him before continuing.

"We trust in God's purpose for our lives," he said, "even when we don't understand. Because of His sovereignty, nothing happens by accident."

He lifted his next point with gentle emphasis. "Point number three is that faith requires action, not superstition. Instead of clinging to good-luck charms, believers cling to the help that comes from God. James, chapter two, verse seventeen, reminds us that *'faith by itself, if it is not accompanied by action, is dead.'* We walk in obedience to Christ. We step forward in faith. And we trust Him with every aspect of our lives. We rely on the promises of Scripture, not the shifting shadows of chance."

"Finally," Pastor Dave said, lifting his eyes from his notes, "point four is that Jesus is our Provider, Protector, and Guide. When we rely on luck, we place our hope in something impersonal and powerless. But when we rely on Jesus, we place our hope in His personal and all-powerful providence."

He flipped a page in his Bible. "In Philippians, chapter four, verse nineteen, Paul assures us, *'And my God will meet all your needs according to the riches of His glory in Christ Jesus.'*

"When you feel lost," he continued gently, "remember Jesus' words in John, chapter fourteen, verse six: *'I am the way and the truth and the life.'* He will guide your steps and provide for your every need, not by chance, but by His love and grace."

Pastor Dave paused, then leaned forward slightly. "We have to make the choice to trust Him. Psalm, chapter thirty-seven, verse five, encourages us: *'Commit your way to the Lord; trust in Him, and He will act.'*"

He closed his Bible and lifted his hands. "Pray with me," he invited.

"Heavenly Father, thank You for being our unshakable foundation. Teach us to trust You fully and reject the false security of luck. May we walk by faith, not by sight, and rely on Your promises for every step we take. In Jesus' name, Amen."

The choir immediately began the familiar, soothing tune of "Tis So Sweet to Trust in Jesus," and the congregation rose to sing. Voices blended in warm harmony, filling the sanctuary with comfort and conviction. Shaya sang along, her heart swelling with peace.

When the song ended, Pastor Dave returned to the pulpit. He scanned the congregation with gentle seriousness.

"Some of you here today," he said, "need to place your trust in the Living God. You have been relying on luck for too long, and it has let you down time and time again. If you need to accept Christ as your Lord and Savior, if you are ready to dedicate your life to Him, please repeat after me. Everyone, bow your heads."

Shaya lowered her head again.

"Jesus," Pastor Dave prayed, "I know that I am a sinner. I believe that You died on the cross and conquered death by rising again. I declare You to be Lord of my life as I surrender to Your will. Please forgive me of my sins. Thank You for Your grace and mercy. In Jesus' name, Amen."

As the final "Amen" echoed through the sanctuary, Shaya lifted her head and froze. Her father's head was still bowed. His shoulders trembled with a slow breath, and his hands were clasped tightly in front of him.

Did he just pray with the pastor? Her heartbeat quickened. *Could he have dedicated his life to God?* If he had, it would be one of the greatest blessings she'd witnessed in a long time. She tucked the moment deep into her heart, already planning to talk to him later.Rance was unusually quiet on the drive to Attie's house. The sun filtered through the windshield, warming his face, but his mind churned with thoughts he wasn't ready to voice, not in the car, not in motion. *Maybe over lunch,* he thought. *Some things deserve a real conversation.*

Once inside, they settled at the kitchen table. The scent of brewed coffee drifted between them. Attie studied him for a long moment, concern softening her expression. She reached across the table and placed her hand on top of his.

"You've been awfully quiet since church," she said gently.

Rance looked down at their hands for a moment before smiling faintly. "I've been mulling a lot over in my head," he admitted. "I was really moved by the pastor's message today."

Attie's face brightened. "It *was* an incredible sermon," she said, squeezing his hand with encouragement.

Rance cleared his throat, his voice gentle but steady. "I realized this morning that my whole life has been based on what *I* wanted. I never considered God's will for me. It really made me think. But . . . it wasn't just that." He looked down at his hands, then back up at her. "I . . . well, I decided to . . . I gave my life to God this morning."

Attie screeched a joyful, unrestrained sound and shot out of her chair so fast it toppled over behind her. "Hallelujah!" she shouted, bouncing up and down like a child receiving the best gift imaginable. "Rance, that is *so* amazing! I'm so happy!"

Rance's face flushed, but his eyes shone. "I am too, Attie. I feel different, you know? And it feels good." He stood, righted her chair, then took both her hands in his. His thumbs brushed lightly over her fingers.

"Attie," he said quietly, "how would you feel about me moving back permanently? What if I could work something out with the Bureau so I could stay here with you? And Shaya and our grandbaby.

Attie . . . I love you, and I don't want to rely on luck anymore. I want God to guide my path . . . with you."

Attie's eyes filled instantly. "Oh, Rance," she breathed, "you have no idea how long I have waited to hear those words. I would *love* to have you stay."

He inhaled slowly. "I don't have a ring. And maybe it's too soon to talk about this." His voice dipped to a whisper. "But I would really like for you to be my wife again."

"Yes," Attie said without a pause. She threw her arms around him. "I will marry you. You don't need a new ring. I still have the one you gave me in the beginning."

"You kept that?" Rance asked, stunned. "I thought that would've been thrown out years ago."

"I never gave up hope," Attie said softly as she pulled away. "I'll be right back."

She dashed into her bedroom. The sound of rummaging echoed down the hall as she dug through her jewelry drawer. Finally, she found what she was looking for: the wedding set she had never been able to part with. She hurried back to the kitchen, her hands trembling with excitement.

"See?" she said, holding it out.

Rance took the rings reverently, then lifted her left hand. "Well then," he murmured, "let's put this ring back where it belongs." He slid the bands onto her finger with slow, steady care. "There. That's better."

Attie lifted her hand, letting the light catch the princess-cut diamond. "It's more beautiful now than it was thirty years ago," she whispered. She looked up at Rance, her smile glowing with youthful joy. He leaned in and kissed her gently.

Attie pulled back with a gasp. "Let's call Pastor Dave and see when he's available. Is tomorrow too soon?"

Rance laughed, the sound warm and full. "Attie girl, I think we need to get a license first." He kissed her again, quick and affectionate.

"But I'll marry you as soon as we can make it happen. Should we call our daughter?"

Attie paused, thinking. Then she shook her head with a grin. "No, not yet. Let's enjoy being engaged for a moment." She slid her arms around his neck, resting her forehead against his. "I love you, Rance. I always have."

CHAPTER TWENTY-SIX

The next morning, Attie and Rance arrived at the courthouse the moment the doors opened. The process was quick, almost shockingly so, and within minutes they stepped back out into the sunlight with a marriage license in hand. They walked to the car grinning like teenagers, fingers laced tightly together.

As soon as Attie sat down, she pulled out her phone. She couldn't wait one more second. She called Pastor Dave's office, bouncing her heel against the floor while she waited for someone to pick up. After a brief conversation, full of excitement on her end and warm amusement on his, Pastor Dave agreed to marry them that very night.

When Rance pulled up to her house to drop her off before heading in to work, he turned to her with raised brows. "Are you sure you don't want more time to prepare something more elaborate?"

Attie shook her head firmly. "I have our rings, and most importantly, I have you. That's all I need."

Rance smiled, but still asked, "What if the kids can't come?"

"Then Jessie, Katie, or Joe will record it," Attie said without hesitation. "I am marrying you tonight. Don't try to back out on me."

Rance laughed and squeezed her hand. "I love you, Attie. And you can't get rid of me that easily this time."

She leaned over, kissed him, and hopped out of the car. As she walked toward the house, she waved at him and called, "I'll see you tonight!" She practically floated up her front steps. Time for phone calls.

Her first call was to Shaya.

"Hi, Mom," Shaya answered breathlessly, "can I call you back? I'm swamped."

Attie barreled ahead. "No need! You and Ben come to the church tonight at five-thirty. Bring a side dish."

"What are you talking about?" Shaya demanded. "What are you up to?"

"Nothing! Just be there with a side dish. Oh, and call Jexi. Tell her and Hunter to come too. See you tonight!"

"Mom . . . ."

Click.

Attie didn't have time to field objections. Shaya would figure it out later. Besides, she knew her daughter well enough to know Shaya wouldn't miss it.

Next, Attie called her sisters and brother, giving each one the same vague-but-cheerful instructions. Each hung up sounding equally confused. Attie couldn't help smiling at their bafflement. Then she gasped. *The ham!* The one in her freezer would never thaw in time. She needed a fresh one.

"And flowers," she added to herself, already grabbing her purse. "A bride needs flowers."

The rest of the day went by in a whirlwind. At home, she found a dress tucked in the back of her closet, a lovely light-teal, knee-length dress with a lace overlay. Not formal, but elegant. Exactly right for a simple, meaningful ceremony. She paired it with the small bouquet of cream-colored roses she bought and laid everything out with a satisfied sigh.

That evening, family members trickled into the sanctuary, murmuring among themselves.

"Why the side dish?"

"What's going on?"

"Did someone win something?"

Shaya and Ben sat with Hunter and Jexi, exchanging theories. But before they could settle on one, the doors opened.

Rance and Attie entered hand in hand.

Shaya blinked. Her mother's smile was luminous, brighter than she had seen in years.

Rance cleared his throat. "Everyone, thank you for coming tonight under such cryptic circumstances." He looked at Attie, then back at their family. "I want to share that I surrendered my life to Christ yesterday . . . and I also asked Attie to remarry me."

Gasps. Cheers. And a few teary laughs.

"She said yes," Rance added, "and Pastor Dave has agreed to perform the ceremony right now."

The room erupted.

"Congratulations!"

"That's amazing!"

"Praise God!"

Shaya rushed forward and wrapped both her parents in a hug. "I'm thrilled for you both! But, what about Dane and Ronan? Are they coming?"

Attie brushed a hand over Shaya's cheek. "I called them. They're very happy for us, but they're too far away to get here tonight."

"You don't want to wait until they can come?" Shaya asked, eyebrows raised.

"We'll send them the video," Attie said, smiling. "I want to do this now. I'm done waiting."

Shaya exhaled, then grinned. "Oh . . . well then. Congrats!"

After all the others had shared hugs and well wishes, Rance yelled out above the noise, "Let's get this show on the road!"

Everyone laughed and quieted, and Pastor Dave took his place at the podium. "Please come join me, Attie and Rance."

"WAIT!" Attie exclaimed. "I need my flowers. Shay, can you run get them on the table outside the door? I didn't want to give away the surprise by walking in with them."

Shaya retrieved the flowers and handed them to her mother. She leaned in and kissed her on the cheek before she found her seat next to Ben.

As she turned, Jessie caught her hand and gave it a gentle squeeze. "She's really happy," Jessie whispered.

Shaya nodded, her throat tight. "She really is."

The rest of the family members took seats in the pews while Rance and Attie joined Pastor Dave at the front of the church. The entire ceremony was short, and afterward, Pastor Dave announced, "By the power vested in me, I now present to you, Mr. and Mrs. Rance Clark!"

Cheers erupted and Rance leaned down and kissed Attie. Shaya wiped tears from her eyes as Ben wrapped his arm around her shoulders. He leaned over to whisper in her ear, "I did not see that coming."

"Me either!" Shaya said. "But I have to admit, it's an answer to a prayer I've been praying for years."

Rance declared, "Let's eat!" and they all filed out of the sanctuary to the fellowship hall for the makeshift reception.

While they were eating, Attie looked over at Rance. "I do have one question," she said. "What are you going to do about your position with the FBI? Won't they be expecting you back after you finish this case?"

Rance grinned at her. "Attie, my love, I have all of that worked out! I spoke with my supervisor today. Because of the cleaning up we've been doing at the Joplin PD, the department is in need of a new police chief. My boss is giving me that position so that I can stay here permanently!"

Attie's eyes rounded with shock. "Won't that be like a demotion?" she asked.

"Who cares?" Rance said with a laugh. "I have everything I ever need or want. It's just a job and I know God will provide for us. I'm not concerned about my career or the extra money. It's not important to me anymore." He put his hand on hers. "Baby, I'm never leaving you again."

Attie melted into his arms. "I'm proud of you, Rance Clark," she said as she leaned her head on his shoulder. "You are quite a man. And I am so glad you're mine."

CHAPTER TWENTY-SEVEN

In Honduras, Sebastian was making preparations to move to the United States. Rance had arranged for him to live in the upstairs apartment above Katie's Diner for a while, until he could find a permanent place. He was mostly packed and his tickets had already been purchased. The only thing that he regretted is that his mama wouldn't be coming with him. He had tried to convince her to come, but she had refused.

The night before his flight was to leave, he went to her house for dinner.

"Mama," he said after they had eaten, "you always cook the best food. Are you sure you don't want to come to the United States with me? I will miss your cooking!"

His mother threw a hot pad in his direction. "Just miss my cooking?" she asked, laughing.

"Of course, I will miss you," Sebastian answered. "That is why you need to come with me! You would love it!"

"Sebastian, *mijo,* I love you," she said in broken English. "But my life here. This is the only home I know."

"But after I go, who will take care of you?" Sebastian asked. "Who will keep you company?"

"Lucinda next door is a good girl," his mother said. "She take care of me. She help me a lot. You do not worry." She stepped closer and cupped his face in her hands. "My baby boy is leaving the nest. This important to you, you must go!"

Sebastian's eyes misted with tears. "I love you, Mama," he said as he hugged her. "I will call you all the time."

"I love you, *mijo,"* his mother replied. "I am so happy for you. You make your mother proud. Go get that girl and marry her. I need *nietos.* Give me grandbabies before I die!"

Sebastian pulled back and looked at the ground. "Mama," he said embarrassed. "You won't die anytime soon. And I don't know if Harli feels that way about me."

His mother smiled and winked. "A mama knows," she said. "You fly me there for the wedding."

Sebastian laughed. "Okay, Mama. I can't tell you no." He stepped closer to hug her again. "My plane leaves in the morning. Do you need anything before I go?"

"Call me before you leave," his mother answered. She turned away, and he saw that she was beginning to cry.

"Oh, Mama," he said softly. "This is so difficult. It's so hard to leave you."

"You make me proud, *mi hijo,"* his mother repeated. "I brag about you to all the neighbors. Now, go get some rest before your plane."

"I will call you every single day. *Te amo,* Mama, I love you," Sebastian said as he walked out the door.

"Yo también te amo," his mother said in return.

As promised, Rance had a rental car waiting for Sebastian when he disembarked the plane the following day. He entered the address into his GPS and started on his way to a new beginning. "Thank you, Abba, for this opportunity." He prayed aloud. "I will continue to follow where You lead. And if Harli is in my future . . ." He smiled. "I won't be upset."

No, he wouldn't be upset at all.

The time flew by as he drove to Baxter Springs. Once at the apartment, he unpacked his few belongings and glanced around. This place would be perfect for the time being. It didn't hurt that he'd be living right above a diner.

He called his mother to let her know he'd arrived safely. After hanging up, he snapped a few pictures to send her so she could see that he was comfortable. Then he called Harli to tell her he'd made it to the States.

Harli answered after the second ring, "Hello there!"

Sebastian couldn't hide the smile in his voice. "Hi!" he returned. "Guess where I am right now?"

"Hmm, I don't know," Harli answered. "Do I really have to guess?"

"I made it to Baxter Springs!" Sebastian said cheerfully. "I'm getting settled in the apartment."

"That's great!" Harli almost squealed.

Did he hear a hint of excitement in her voice? His heart flipped a little in his chest.

Harli continued. "I'll have some free time in about a week. I can come for another visit if you'd like. I'd like to see Shaya and Jexi again!"

"I'd love to see you!" Sebastian said. "I'm not sure what my schedule will be at the department yet. Can I let you know which days I will be available?"

"Of course," Harli said. "My schedule is far more flexible than yours. Especially with you being the newbie. And now that you're Stateside, it'll be easier to spend time together."

Sebastian chose his words carefully. "Harli, I am very serious about wanting to start a relationship with you." He took a breath and continued. "If that is too fast, I'm sorry. But you deserve to know how I feel and I came here to prove it."

Harli paused before responding. "Sebastian, we've known each other for a long time, but we haven't really had the chance to *know* each other. I can't deny that I care about you. I just want more time together so we can be sure we want to pursue this."

"I disagree," Sebastian said. "I feel like we do know each other quite well. What about all the hours we've spent on the phone and video chatting? You know me. I know you."

"True," Harli said. "During those hours, I've told you things I don't tell just anyone. We *have* grown closer. But can we see how things feel next week when I come up?"

"As long as I know you're open to an *us*, that's all I'm asking," Sebastian said. "For now."

Harli cleared her throat. "I have to admit that I get butterflies when it comes to you," she confessed. "I just want to make sure that we don't move too fast."

"We will take as much time as you need," Sebastian said. "I'm not going anywhere. I truly believe God led us to each other."

Harli chuckled, a little uncomfortably. "You don't think it could've just been a happy coincidence?" she asked.

"I don't believe in coincidences anymore," Sebastian replied.

"Well, okay, but how do you know God was involved?" Harli asked. "Shaya asked me to help with the Juan Carlos situation, which is ultimately how we met."

Sebastian sighed. "I know, but who do you think gave Shaya the idea to call you?" he asked. "I'm not trying to push you, but I'd like you to consider that God may have orchestrated it."

"So, you're saying God orchestrated the kidnapping so that we could meet?" Harli asked, sarcasm creeping into her voice.

The conversation was going wrong fast.

"I believe God allows things to happen," Sebastian said carefully. "And He can bring good out of terrible situations."He heard her scoff softly on the other end. "Whatever, Sebastian. Let's just agree to disagree."

Panic tightened in his chest. This wasn't how he'd imagined this conversation going. He tried to recover.

"Harli, let's not argue. I'm sorry if I upset you," he said quickly. "Let's just focus on next week. I'll send you my schedule as soon as I can."

Her voice softened. "Okay. That sounds good," she said. "I've got an appointment soon. I'll talk to you later."

After the call disconnected, Sebastian closed his eyes and whispered a prayer. "Lord, open her eyes to Your truth. I know she believes in You, but she struggles to see Your love and power. Please show her."

CHAPTER TWENTY-EIGHT

Selena's graduation from high school soon arrived and Jessie busied herself planning her party to celebrate. She was proud of the young lady that Selena was becoming and how well she was handling everything. The girl had continued going to church and pursuing a relationship with God and had become more convinced that giving her baby to Shaya and Ben was His plan.

Jessie had rapidly grown to love Selena as her own daughter and the two had formed a strong bond.

Jessie spoke with Katie and arranged for several of Selena's favorite foods. She bought decorations, ordered a cake, and invited a few friends Selena had made at school.

On the day of the party, Jessie rose early to decorate the house. She placed cutouts of graduation hats all over the living room and kitchen. She hung streamers in the doorways and set up the table with snacks and drinks. She even had glitter confetti to shake all over the table.

Midmorning, she left to pick up the cake. When she returned, Selena was sitting in the living room watching television. Jessie set the cake on the table and joined her on the couch.

"Hey there, graduation girl," Jessie said softly. "Ready for today?"

Selena turned to Jessie. "Sort of," she replied.

"Sort of?" Jessie asked. "What do you mean? Is something wrong?"

Selena lowered her eyes. "Well, I am beginning to show a little bit and I have not told my friends about the baby. Deena mentioned the other day that the shirt that I was wearing made me look pregnant. I do not think that she was trying to be mean, but I did not know what to say."

Jessie pulled her into a hug, then leaned back and met her eyes. "You don't owe anyone an explanation," she said gently. "But you also don't need to be ashamed if you choose to be honest. If she says something again, you can tell her her words are hurtful, not helpful. Either way, the choice is yours."

"I'll have to tell them eventually," Selena said. "I'm just afraid they'll stop being my friends."

Jessie nodded. "I understand that fear. I've learned that people who are meant to stay, people God wants in your life, will stay. Some won't, and that hurts. But the true friends always do."

The doorbell rang and Jessie checked her watch. "Right on time," she said as she stood to answer the door.

Selena jumped up. "I'm not ready! Who could be here already?" She rushed off to her room to change.

Jessie opened the door and smiled brightly. "Mayella! Tomas! I'm so glad you made it." She knelt to greet the children. "You must be Rio. And you're Adan! Come in, all of you."

As the family settled into the living room, Mayella thanked Jessie quietly. Jessie assured them Selena would be out shortly.

Jessie knocked on Selena's door. "Almost ready?"

"Just a minute!" Selena called.

"Hurry," Jessie said with a smile. "I have a surprise for you."

Back in the living room, Jessie chatted with Tomas about their flight and rental car.

"We are very grateful," Tomas said. "Thank you for arranging everything."

Selena's voice drifted down the hallway. "Who's here?"

She stepped into the living room and froze. Her eyes widened, and for a moment she couldn't speak.

"Papa . . . Mama?" she whispered. "Rio? Adan?"

Mayella leapt up and wrapped Selena in her arms, tears spilling freely. *"Mi niña,"* she cried.

"Mama," Selena sobbed. "I've missed you so much."

Tomas joined them, holding his daughter close. "Our baby girl," he said softly.

After a moment, Selena rushed to her siblings, hugging and kissing them as they giggled and darted away from her grasp.

Jessie wiped at her own tears and approached Tomas. "I'm glad you could come," she said.

"We couldn't have without you," he replied. "Thank you for everything. For caring for our daughter. We owe you so much."

"You don't owe me anything," Jessie said. "I'm just glad I could help."

Selena hugged Jessie tightly. "Thank you. This means more than you know."

"Today's yours," Jessie said softly.

"Wait!" Selena suddenly exclaimed. She ran to her room and returned, waving a letter. "I got accepted to the nursing program!" she shouted. "Missouri Southern State University. I'm going to college!"

Cheers erupted, hugs followed, and Selena's face ached from smiling. She rested a hand on her stomach and thought, *Not even this situation would change a thing.*

Soon, other guests began arriving to honor Selena, and the house filled with laughter and music. Jessie turned on a playlist of upbeat songs, and the living room buzzed with conversation. Selena's friends gathered around her, talking about their future plans.

Katie arrived with trays of food, and the kitchen quickly became crowded as everyone sampled Selena's favorite dishes. The smell of warm spices and fresh bread filled the house. Rio and Adan darted between guests, occasionally stopping to steal a cookie before being gently scolded by Mayella.

Selena opened cards and gifts in the living room, her smile growing with each one. She couldn't ever remember feeling this happy and this loved.

As the party wound down, Selena joined Jessie in the kitchen.

"I can never repay you for all you have done," Selena said quietly.

"You don't have to," Jessie replied. "One day, you'll pay it forward." She paused, emotion thick in her voice. "Truthfully, I should be thanking you."

"Why?"

Jessie wiped her eyes. "I never had the chance to be a mother. You've allowed me to be one to you."

Selena kissed her cheek. "I love you. You *are* a mother to me."

They hugged, then laughed softly as they looked at the pile of dishes.

"That's a lot of cleanup," Selena said.

"Go be with your family," Jessie replied. "I've got this."

As Selena walked away, Jessie picked up the first dish and let the tears fall. "Thank You, Lord," she whispered, "for sending Selena to me."

CHAPTER TWENTY-NINE

When Selena was twenty-four weeks along, Shaya and Ben attended her prenatal appointment with her. As the doctor performed the sonogram, he nodded and grinned.

"Everything looks wonderful, Selena," he said.

He held the wand in one spot for a moment. "Strong heartbeat, all ten fingers and toes, and growing right on schedule."

Ben looked at the screen. "Um, Doc," he said. "What is that?" He extended his finger toward the monitor. "Is that the umbilical cord?"

Dr. Daniel laughed. "No, son. That isn't the umbilical cord."

Ben's expression changed to acknowledgement. "OH!" he exclaimed.

Shaya's face turned red with embarrassment. "Is that what I think it is?" she asked.

Selena looked at Ben and Shaya and giggled. "That means the baby is a boy!" she exclaimed.

"Well," Ben said, shaking his head with a grin, "so much for not finding out the gender."

Shaya smiled. "At least now we can plan a little better," she said. "And start thinking about names."

After the appointment, Shaya dropped Selena off at Jessie's house and headed into work. She floated through the rest of the day, barely touching the ground. The idea of a little boy filled her with excitement, and she counted the minutes until her shift ended. She wanted to stop by the bookstore and pick up a few books about raising sons.

When she walked into Baxter's Books, she was surprised to see Jexi at the manager's desk, focused on the computer.

"You're working late," Shaya said, approaching her.

Jexi glanced up. "Yeah. There's a lot to get done," she said. "Besides, I hate going home to an empty house."

Shaya noticed her red, swollen eyes and hurried to her side. "What's wrong?" she asked.

"Nothing," Jexi said quickly. "It's no big deal. How did Selena's appointment go?"

"Yes, it *is* a big deal," Shaya insisted. "If it makes you cry, it matters. The update can wait."

Jexi gave a weak smile. "You caught that, huh?"

"I'm not blind," Shaya said dramatically.

Jexi sighed. "Hunter's been working nonstop. He's hardly ever home and never in time for dinner. And when he is home, he's exhausted and doesn't want to talk. I just . . . feel lonely."

Shaya pulled her into a hug, then stepped back. "Have you told him how you're feeling?" she asked gently.

"Of course not," Jexi said. "You know how much his job means to him. He loves what he does. And he'll probably just say that spring and summer are the busiest times for an electrician."

"Jex, your feelings are valid," Shaya said gently. "You need to talk to him. Your marriage is important."

"But so is his job," Jexi protested.

"Not more important than his marriage to you," Shaya said. "Talk to him. Don't be so stubborn. He needs to know what's going on; otherwise, he can't fix it."

Jexi stared at the floor. "Okay. I'll talk to him tonight . . . maybe. If he's not too tired." She lifted her gaze. "Now tell me about the appointment."

"It's a boy!" Shaya whispered excitedly.

Jexi blinked. "I thought you guys weren't going to find out the gender."

"We weren't," Shaya said. "But Ben accidentally spotted the, uh . . . revealing detail on the monitor. Selena pointed it out, and the doctor confirmed it."

Jexi's eyes filled with tears again. "I'm so happy for you!"

"Sure you are," Shaya teased. "You look *thrilled* with tears streaming down your face."

"These are happy tears," Jexi insisted. "I really am happy for you. It's exciting." She wiped her cheeks. "I needed some good news. Have you picked a name yet?"

"Not yet," Shaya said. "And I know you're happy for me, but I can also tell when you're hurting. That's what best friends do."

"Don't make it weird," Jexi said with a small laugh.

Shaya grinned. "Okay. Want more good news? I came in to get some parenting books. Want to help me?"

"Does a cat sleep all day?" Jexi exclaimed. "Of course, I want to help!" She grabbed a tissue, wiped her eyes, and blew her nose. "Come on, follow me."

An hour and seven books later, Shaya stood at the checkout counter. The part-time employee, Brian, scanned the stack and asked casually, "Having a baby?"

"Sort of," Shaya replied with a smile.

Brian glanced at her, puzzled, but didn't ask any follow-up questions. As he was about to tell her the total, Jexi hollered from across the room, "Give her the employee discount, Brian!"

"But she doesn't work here," Brian said slowly.

"She's family," Jexi insisted. "Just do it, please."

"Okay," Brian said, tapping a few buttons before giving Shaya the new total.

Shaya took the bag of books, and Jexi met her at the front door. She pulled her into a hug.

"I am *so* excited for you," Jexi said. "I can't wait to spoil my little nephew! You'll need to name him soon so I can start calling him by name when I see Selena."

"We'll pick one soon, I'm sure," Shaya said, patting the bag. "I've got a baby-name book about a mile thick to get through first. But we might not tell anyone until he's born." She winked. "You won't forget to talk to Hunter tonight, will you?"

"As soon as you pick a name, you *have* to tell me," Jexi whined. "I'm your best friend!"

"Only if you promise to talk to Hunter," Shaya said, raising an eyebrow.

"Fine," Jexi relented. "I'll talk to him."

Shaya headed home, and Jexi began closing up for the night.

"Brian, I'm leaving you to lock up," Jexi said. "Don't forget to set the alarm."

"Yes, Mrs. Bennett," Brian replied.

Jexi checked her watch as she walked to her car. There was still plenty of time to cook dinner for Hunter. She placed her phone in the holder and used the voice command to call him.

When he answered on the third ring, she said, "Hi, babe. I'm leaving the bookstore. What time will you be home?"

Hunter sounded rushed. "Jex, I'm not sure," he said. "I'm still working on the project for Woods Construction, and we're up against a deadline."

Jexi had no response. The words sat heavy in her chest, and she felt completely defeated.

"Babe?" Hunter asked. "Are you still there?"

"Yeah," Jexi said quietly. "Hunter, we really need to talk. Is there any way you could come home for dinner tonight?"

"You're scaring me," Hunter said. "Are you okay?"

"I just need to talk to you," she repeated. "Please."

Hunter paused. "Let me see what I can do," he said. "Maybe Scott can handle things without me for a bit."

"Thank you," Jexi said, her voice wavering as tears stung her eyes. "I love you so much."

"I love you too, Jex," Hunter replied. "Give me an hour to wrap up a few loose ends, okay?"

"Okay," she said softly. "I'll see you at home."

Jexi ended the call and spent the rest of the drive mentally preparing for the conversation ahead. She wasn't ready to talk about it. Not really. But she couldn't keep putting it off.

Guilt pressed at her chest. She hadn't been entirely honest with Shaya earlier. Yes, Hunter's work schedule was part of the problem . . . but there was something else. Something bigger.

CHAPTER THIRTY

Jexi settled on spaghetti for dinner. It was quick and simple, exactly what she needed right now. Her heart felt heavy with loneliness and worry. She was more than a little afraid that Hunter wouldn't have the time or the emotional space to be the source of comfort and reassurance she craved.

Hunter walked in shortly after she finished boiling the noodles. He crossed to the saucepan of meat sauce and lifted the lid.

"Mmm," he said, inhaling deeply. "That smells wonderful."

"Thanks," Jexi said. "You timed it perfectly. It's ready." She served the spaghetti and set the plates on the table, not bothering to mask her mood.

Hunter immediately sensed something was wrong. He stepped closer, pulling her into a hug and brushing a soft kiss against her cheek.

"Jex, are you okay?"

She stiffened in his arms. "Not really," she admitted, stepping away. "We should eat before it gets cold."

Her distance unsettled him. This wasn't like her. Hunter sat down but made no move to pick up his fork.

"We have a microwave," he said gently. "Dinner can wait. Sit down. What did you want to talk about?"

Jexi lowered herself into her chair. She picked up the napkin from the table and twisted it between her fingers, tightening the fabric until it wrinkled and bunched. Before she could speak, tears spilled down her cheeks. Finally, she looked up at him.

"I'm scared, Hunter."

Concern creased his brow. "What's going on?"

"I need you here," she said, her voice trembling. "You've been at work all the time. We barely see each other anymore." She swallowed hard. "Are you trying to avoid me?"

"What? Where is this coming from?" Hunter asked. "I thought we talked about needing extra money. I'm just trying to provide for us."

Jexi tightened the napkin again, twisting it until her knuckles whitened. "How many evenings have we really spent together in the past three weeks?" she asked. "I mean actually sat down and talked as opposed to catching each other for five minutes before falling asleep?" She let out a shaky breath. "I'll answer for you. None."

Hunter opened his mouth to argue, but the words died there. She was right. He reached across the table and took her hand, gently prying the napkin from her grip.

"You're right," he admitted quietly. "I have been at work every evening. I just . . . I thought you were okay with it since you've been staying busy at the bookstore."

"I'm only staying at the bookstore so late because I don't want to come home to an empty house," Jexi said. Her voice cracked. "My employees are perfectly capable of handling the evenings; we're not even that busy." She gave a weak, humorless laugh. "Maybe I should just get a dog."

"Okay," Hunter said quickly. "We can get a dog." He softened. "But more than that, I promise I'll be here more. I didn't know you felt this way. I'm so sorry." His voice dropped. "You *are* my first priority. I guess I haven't been showing you that."

He pushed his chair back and knelt in front of her, wrapping his arms around her waist and resting his head against her chest.

"Thank you," Jexi whispered, tears spilling again as she rested her hands on his shoulders. "I'm going to need you here . . . because there's more."

Hunter lifted his head, concern sharpening his expression. "More?"

"Remember my appointment with Dr. Daniel on Monday?"

"Of course," Hunter said. "Just a routine checkup, right?"

Jexi nodded slowly. "Mostly. But he had some . . . concerns."

Hunter's stomach tightened. "Concerns about what?"

She squeezed her eyes shut. "I don't know how to say this." Her voice broke completely. "He found something. A mass near my spine."

Hunter froze.

"He wants me to see a surgeon next week," she continued, barely able to get the words out. "For more tests."

Hunter jumped up, pulling Jexi to her feet and wrapping her in a fierce hug. "Okay," he said softly. "Where in your back? Show me."

Jexi stepped out of his arms and turned around. She lifted the back of her shirt slightly and pointed to a spot on the left side of her spine, just above her waistband. "Right here."

Hunter placed his palm gently over the area. "Does it hurt?"

"A little," she admitted. "It's manageable. Mostly it tingles or feels numb." She took a steadying breath. "Dr. Daniel is worried that it could eventually cause loss of movement or affect my organs. If it grows, it could press against, or attach to, my spine."

Hunter swallowed.

"He wants me to have a biopsy," she continued. "That's the part I'm scared of. They have to use a large needle to remove tissue."

"Does he think it's cancer?" Hunter asked quietly.

"He doesn't have an opinion yet," Jexi said. "But even if it isn't, it will probably need to be surgically removed." She turned to face him again. "I'll know more after I meet with the surgeon."

Hunter pulled her back into his arms. "I am right here with you, every step of the way," he said firmly. "I'll take time off work. I'm not going anywhere." He rested his forehead against hers. "Come here. Let's pray."

After he finished praying, Jexi melted into his embrace. The loneliness that had weighed on her for weeks finally loosened its grip. For the first time in a long while, she felt like she had her husband back.

She tilted her face up toward him. "Are you scared?"

"A little," Hunter admitted. "But I also know the God we serve is bigger than any mass. I believe He will heal you. I'm choosing trust over fear."

"I wish I had your confidence," Jexi said softly. "I know God is in control. I know I'm held in the palm of His hand. I'm just . . . afraid of what this journey might look like."

"We don't even know if it's something serious yet," Hunter said gently. "It could be something simple, a surgery with no complications."

"My strong pillar of faith," Jexi said with a small grin. "What would I do without you? I love you."

"Thankfully, you'll never have to find out," Hunter replied. He kissed her forehead. "But you'd probably still be just fine. You're stronger than you realize." He patted his stomach. "That said, my belly is empty and significantly less brave. Shall we eat?"

Jexi laughed, the sound lighter than it had been all evening. "You bet. I'm hungry too. We'll just have to reheat everything."

They warmed their plates in the microwave one at a time, then settled back at the table to finish their meal. With the earlier heaviness lifted, they finally relaxed and enjoyed catching up on their week.

Midbite, Jexi dropped her fork and screeched, "Oh, biscuits! I can't believe I forgot to tell you the big news of the day. Ben and Shaya's baby is a boy!"

Hunter laughed. "That's great! I bet Ben is thrilled to have a little man."

"They would've been equally thankful either way," Jexi said. "Shaya told me they found out by accident, but she's glad they know. It'll make shopping and planning easier."

After the dishes were loaded into the dishwasher, Hunter nudged her gently. "You should call your parents. They'll want to know, even if it turns out to be nothing."

"You're right," Jexi admitted. "They'd be furious if I didn't tell them. Okay. I'll call them now."

Hunter headed toward the living room. "I'll be watching football if you need me."

Jexi dialed her parents' number. Her father answered on the third ring.

"Jexi!" he exclaimed. "Our favorite daughter!"

Jexi laughed. "I'm your only daughter, Dad."

"You're still my favorite," he said warmly. "How are you, honey?"

"Is Mom around?" Jexi asked. "I need to talk to you both."

"She's right here. I'll put you on speaker." A brief pause followed. "Okay, Jex, you're on. Your mom is here."

"Hey, Mama," Jexi said.

"Hi, sweetie," her mother replied. "How's everything going?"

"A little wild and crazy," Jexi admitted. "Remember how I told you Ben and Shaya are adopting a baby? They found out it's a boy! Isn't that exciting?"

"What wonderful news," her mother said. "I'm sure they're over the moon."

"They are," Jexi said. "I helped Shaya pick out some baby books tonight."

"Well, that's incredible," her dad chimed in.

A quiet beat passed before her mother spoke again. "Jexi . . . what else is going on? I can hear it in your voice."

"Really, Mom?" Jexi sighed. "Why does there have to be anything else?"

"A mother knows."

Jexi hesitated, then exhaled. "Okay . . . the truth is, I have a small mass near my spine. I'm meeting with a surgeon next week for a biopsy and to talk through options."

"Jexi!" her mother shrieked. "I'm coming to you right away!"

"No, there's no need," Jexi insisted. "Hunter is here, and we don't know anything yet. It could be nothing."

"A mass near your spine doesn't sound like nothing," her father said gently.

"Let me hear what the doctor says next week first, okay?" Jexi pleaded.

Her mother relented with a shaky breath. "All right. But call me the minute you get any news."

Jexi ended the call and set her phone on the table, exhaling slowly. For a moment, she just stared at the dark screen, her reflection faint and tired. *I shouldn't have told them tonight*, she thought. *But they deserved to know.*

Her chest tightened. *A mass near my spine.* The words echoed like something spoken by someone else, about someone else. She rubbed her arms, suddenly chilled. *What if it's nothing? What if it's something?* The questions chased each other in circles, offering no comfort.

She could hear the faint sound of the football game from the living room. Hunter's steady presence, grounding her even from a distance. *At least I'm not facing this alone,* she reminded herself. And next week . . . next week I'll have some answers.

Still, as she stood and walked toward the living room, a quiet whisper lingered in the back of her mind: *Please, God . . . let it be nothing.*

CHAPTER THIRTY-ONE

Jexi anxiously awaited Shaya's arrival at Punkins Place. This little coffee shop had become one of her favorites since moving to Baxter Springs. The owner loved Jesus and shared that love in her coffee and treats.

Jexi kept glancing toward the door, her stomach twisting every time it opened. *She's still upset*, Jexi thought. *And who could blame her? I practically hung up on her yesterday.* But she knew she'd made the right call. This wasn't news you delivered over the phone.

Shaya finally stepped inside, spotted her, and headed straight to the table. She slid into the seat across from her and clasped her hands on the table, her expression tight.

"What is it that you couldn't tell me on the phone?" she quipped, though her tone carried more edge than humor.

"I know that upset you," Jexi began, her voice soft. "And I'm sorry. But I wanted to tell you face-to-face."

"Okay," Shaya said, leaning forward. "Here's my face."

Jexi drew in a sharp breath. Her heart thudded. *Just say it. Rip the bandage off.*

"I have a spot in my back near my spine."

The irritation on Shaya's face vanished instantly, replaced by concern so deep it made Jexi's throat tighten. She continued, her voice flattening as if detaching would make it easier. "I'm going in on Tuesday for an MRI and CT scan. Then I'll have a biopsy on Friday. We don't know if it's cancerous or not."

Shaya's mouth fell open. For a moment, neither of them spoke.

"What time are your appointments?" Shaya finally asked. "I'm coming with you."

"You don't need to do that," Jexi said quickly. "Hunter will be with me."

"I didn't ask if you wanted me to go," Shaya said firmly. "You don't get a vote. I will be with you, even if it's in the waiting room."

A small grin tugged at Jexi's lips despite the heaviness in her chest. "Thank you."

Shaya reached across the table and grabbed her hand. "We're going to get through this."

"Don't make it weird," Jexi giggled, grateful for the moment of levity.

Shaya smiled. "I will make it weird when it comes to your health. You are my best friend, and you are not doing this without me."

"I appreciate that," Jexi said. *More than you know.* "I wouldn't want to do this without you. Or Hunter."

Shaya squeezed her hand. "Or God. We don't have to do anything without God."

"Absolutely!" Jexi exclaimed, feeling a flicker of comfort.

Shaya's phone rang. She pulled it from her purse and glanced at the screen. "It's Harli!" She swiped to answer. "Hey, Harli!"

"Hi, Shaya! I'm coming to town next weekend to see Sanchez. I'd love for us all to get together and have dinner."

"We'd love that!" Shaya said. "Aren't you excited he's living here in the States now?"

"Yes, I am," Harli replied. "It makes it a lot easier to visit each other, that's for sure!"

Shaya pulled the phone slightly away from her face and whispered to Jexi, "Harli is coming next weekend. Wants us all to have dinner."

Jexi winced. "I can't promise I'll be there . . . I don't know how I'll feel after the biopsy." *Or if I'll even be in the right headspace,* she added silently.

Shaya returned to the call. "Jexi and Hunter might not be able to make it, but we'll play it by ear," she told Harli. "You're staying with us, right? You can't stay with Sanchez, and I won't let you stay in a hotel! Ben and I have plenty of space!"

"Oh, I don't want to intrude on you guys," Harli said. "I'll be fine in a hotel."

"Nonsense!" Shaya insisted. "The nearest hotel is in Joplin. There's no need for that. You're staying with us."

"Oh, okay. Thank you," Harli said. "I really appreciate it. I plan on leaving Friday around noon, so I should get there around six. Will that mess with your work schedules?"

"Not at all!" Shaya said. "I'll be home by then, and Ben should be too. I'm so excited! I can't wait to see you again!"

"I'm looking forward to it," Harli said. "I'll talk to you later!"

"Bye!" Shaya said, disconnecting the call.

She turned her attention back to Jexi. "Do you think the biopsy is going to be invasive?"

"I guess I don't really know," Jexi replied. "It'll probably depend on the MRI and CT scan results. I know they'll either use a needle to extract tissue or they'll slice me open."

"That's rather dramatic, don't you think?" Shaya snarked.

"If they have to do a surgical biopsy, that's what they'd do," Jexi retorted. "They'll cut right into me!"

Shaya rolled her eyes. "It would be a small incision, I'm sure."

"It's still a cut!" Jexi defended. "With stitches!"

"We'll pray for the needle then," Shaya said.

"Not that the needle will be any better," Jexi muttered.

Shaya softened, her expression gentling. "Jex, I know you're scared, but everything will be okay." She reached for her friend's hand again. "We serve a gigantic, HUGE, powerful God."

Jexi straightened and put her hands on her hips. "I'm not scared," she tried to protest.

"Okay, miss tough girl," Shaya said. "I won't argue. Let's order some lunch."

They placed their orders, and halfway through eating, Shaya paused and looked at her again. "Speaking of important things . . . have you talked to Hunter?"

Jexi nodded. "I did." She lifted a chicken strip and took a bite.

Shaya raised her hands expectantly. "AND?"

"It went well," Jexi said after swallowing.

"Now you're starting to act like me," Shaya scoffed. "You know I want details."

Jexi raised her eyebrows. "Annoying, isn't it?"

Shaya narrowed her eyes in mock irritation. "Fine. Don't tell me. I didn't really want to know anyway."

"Okay," Jexi said, taking another bite of her chicken.

"STOP!" Shaya urged. "I didn't mean it. I have to know!"

"Oh, fine," Jexi relented. "I told him that we really haven't spent any quality time together in quite a while. He said he thought I was happy working late at the bookstore. I told him the only reason I was working late was because I didn't want to be home alone. I even suggested maybe I should get a dog!"

"That's it?" Shaya asked.

"Nah, he actually understood," Jexi said. "He realized he's been working a lot of hours, but it was only to make sure he could provide for us. We're both going to make more of an effort to have at least two nights a week together. Maybe more if we can make it work." She sipped her tea. "In retrospect, the extra money will probably come in handy with the potential medical issue."

"I'm going to claim it right now, in the name of Jesus, that there will be no medical issue," Shaya said firmly. "God is going to heal you, Jex. It's going to be okay."

"But we don't know that," Jexi said gently. "We pray for and want healing, but we don't truly know what God's will is for this situation."

"I know," Shaya admitted. "But that won't stop me from praying for a miracle."

"Me either," Jexi said.

She leaned forward, a twinkle in her eye. "So . . . do you want to go puppy shopping with me?"

"We also need to shop for my son's nursery," Shaya replied, smiling. "How about we plan a shopping trip after we get your biopsy over with and after Harli's visit?"

"Perfect," Jexi said. "That would be perfect."

CHAPTER THIRTY-TWO

Harli arrived Friday evening shortly after six o'clock. Shaya greeted her with a warm hug, and Ben grabbed her suitcase to carry it to the guest room.

"Please let me know if you need anything," Shaya said. "I'm serious."

Harli laughed. "I feel like some important dignitary! But yes, I'll let you know."

"Would you and Sebastian be okay with having dinner here tonight instead of going out?" Shaya asked. "Jexi had a biopsy done today and isn't up to wearing real clothes."

Harli whipped around from where she was unpacking. "Biopsy?!" she gasped. "Why didn't you say anything? Is she okay?"

"Yes, she's okay," Shaya assured her. "We'll fill you in later, but we thought it would be easier and more comfortable for Jexi to come here."

"Of course," Harli said. "We can cancel if she needs to!"

"She wants to see you," Shaya said. "And she doesn't want to be stuck at home if she doesn't have to be."

"Then let's order takeout," Harli suggested. "I don't want you cooking for everyone, and I'm too tired to help."

"I like the way you think!" Shaya said with a grin. She checked her watch. "Hunter and Jexi will be here in about twenty minutes. Can you call Sebastian and tell him to come here instead of the restaurant?"

"Yep," Harli said. "I'll be out shortly!"

Shaya stepped out of the room and closed the door behind her. She found Ben in the kitchen rummaging through cabinets.

"Don't take out any of those pans," she warned. "We are ordering takeout!"

Ben slid the skillet back into the cabinet. "Oh, thank goodness!" he said. "From where?"

"How about that new Chinese restaurant that opened last month?" Shaya suggested. "Would you be willing to go get it when it's ready?"

"Yeah," Ben said. "I'm sure Hunter can go with me to help carry it all. You place the order and let me know when."

Shaya headed to the living room to place the order. She was just finishing up when the doorbell rang.

"Ben," she called, "can you get that, please?"

Ben opened the door to Hunter and Jexi. "You two don't have to ring the bell," he said. "If it's open, come on in! Hunter, don't get comfortable. We're the door-dashers tonight."

Hunter blinked. "Say what?"

Ben laughed. "Shaya's ordering Chinese for everyone, and you and I are picking it up."

"Oh, no problem," Hunter said. "I was worried we were working a new job tonight. I'm really too tired for that."

Harli emerged from the guest room. "Hunter! Jexi!" she said, hurrying over. "So good to see you both!" She hugged them, then settled onto the couch. "Sebastian will be here soon."

Jexi lowered herself gingerly into a chair. "Thank you all for being willing to change our plans at the last minute."

Harli turned toward her. "Of course! How are you feeling, Jexi? Shaya said you had a biopsy but wouldn't give me any more details. Are you okay?"

"I'm tender," Jexi said. "That was a really BIG needle. But I think I'm okay. I had an MRI and a CT scan earlier this week, and the results definitely showed a mass near my spine. We don't know yet if it's cancerous; that's what the biopsy will tell us."

"Oh, Jexi!" Harli exclaimed. "I had no idea you were going through all that. I could have postponed my visit. You should have said something."

"Don't be silly," Jexi replied. "I wanted to see you. And I'm not letting this situation control our lives. I'll be fine. Besides, your visit is primarily for Sebastian anyway. We just get to enjoy your company as an added bonus."

Harli's cheeks flushed crimson. She opened her mouth to respond, but the doorbell rang again.

"And speaking of... !" Shaya said, hurrying to the door. "Sebastian! We were just talking about you! Come on in!"

Sebastian stepped into the living room and gave a tentative wave. "You weren't saying anything bad about me, were you?"

"Of course not!" Shaya answered as she shut the door.

"Hi and bye," Ben said as he and Hunter passed Sebastian in the doorway. "Hunter and I are running to pick up dinner. We'll be back in a few."

Sebastian turned to Harli. "Hi, Harli. It's so nice to see you."

Harli stood. "You, too. You look well."

Shaya snorted. "Oh, cut it out, you two. Hug each other already." She glanced at Jexi. "Hey, Jex, come help me in the kitchen. We need plates and silverware, and we should probably make tea or something."

Jexi looked up, ready to protest, but one look at Shaya's expression shut that down. "Oh, yeah. Coming." She stood slowly and winked at Harli as she headed toward the kitchen.

Harli stepped closer to Sebastian. "It really is good to see you," she said softly.

Sebastian reached for her, and she walked straight into his arms. "I've missed this," he murmured, wrapping her in a warm, familiar embrace.

Harli's breath caught. "I've missed you too." She rested her head against his chest, letting herself remember how safe she always felt there. Her heart fluttered at the thought of him being closer now. Close enough that seeing each other wouldn't require crossing an ocean.

She pulled back, but only slightly, their faces still close as they searched each other's eyes.

"Harli," Sebastian whispered. He leaned in, but she stepped back.

"Don't," she whispered.

Sebastian exhaled, frustrated but gentle. "I know you've been hesitant about us being in a relationship. But I'm living in the States now. We're only six hours apart. Please tell me you've at least considered the possibility of there being an 'us.' You can't deny the chemistry between us."

Harli held his gaze and saw the earnestness there . . . the hope. "I won't lie," she said quietly. "I have thought about it. I do care for you." She swallowed. "I just . . . I don't know if a long-distance relationship can really work."

"Of course it can," Sebastian said. "People do it all the time!" He tilted his head and gave her a wry smile. "It's worth exploring."

"Well, I suppose you're right about us only being six hours apart," Harli said. "Can I think about it?"

"Only as long as your answer is yes," Sebastian teased.

The door swung open as Hunter and Ben returned with the food. "Chow time!" Ben called.

Shaya and Jexi walked in carrying plates and silverware. "Let's eat in the living room," Shaya suggested.

Hunter helped spread the dishes across the coffee table, and everyone served themselves.

After they finished dinner, Sebastian set his plate aside. "How about a rematch of charades?" he asked. "I didn't get to participate in the last game."

"Because you fell asleep!" Harli reminded him.

Everyone laughed.

"As tempting as that sounds," Jexi said, "I don't feel up for charades tonight. But you all go ahead."

Hunter rubbed gentle circles on her back. "We should probably head home soon," he said. "My girl needs to rest."

"Ben and I need to clean up this mess anyway," Shaya said. "Harli, Sebastian, feel free to watch TV or take a walk or something."

Sebastian took Harli's hand. "You know, a walk doesn't sound half bad. I need to walk off all that food."

Harli smiled. "Yeah, I think a walk would be good for both of us."

Sebastian rubbed his belly dramatically. "Are you trying to insinuate something?"

Ben chuckled as he and Shaya headed toward the kitchen. "We'll all be hungry again in an hour anyway."

Harli laughed. "Sebastian, I'm not suggesting anything except that the fresh air will be nice."

"Then let's go for that walk," Sebastian said. He offered his arm, elbow bent in an exaggerated gentlemanly pose. "Mi'lady," he joked.

"Mi'lord," Harli joked back as she took his arm. She called toward the house, "We'll be back soon!" Then she and Sebastian stepped out into the humid night air.

For a few moments, they walked in comfortable silence.

"It's so peaceful here," Harli said at last. "It's so different from Dallas. There's always traffic noise and sirens outside my apartment."

Sebastian stopped walking and turned to face her. "Have you thought about my question?"

Harli stopped too, meeting his eyes. "I have," she said. "I do want a relationship with you, Sebastian . . . but not a long-distance one."

Sebastian's face fell. "I understand."

"So," Harli continued, "I'm going to move to Baxter Springs. Or somewhere nearby."

Sebastian stared at her, stunned. "What? Did I hear you right?"

Harli nodded. "Like I said, Dallas is noisy and chaotic. I want a slower pace of life. And I want a relationship with you. All of that is here."

Sebastian swept her into his arms and spun her in a circle. “You just made me the happiest man alive!”

Harli laughed. “Slow down, cowboy! The happiest man alive? Really?”

Sebastian set her gently back on her feet. “You have no idea. I’ve been crazy about you from the moment I met you.”

“I still have a lot of details to work out before I can move,” Harli said. “But I’m ready to make this a reality.”

Sebastian let out a loud whoop. “Yep, happiest man alive!”

CHAPTER THIRTY-THREE

Jexi was in her office paying invoices and placing new book orders when her cell phone rang. She picked it up and stared at the number on the screen. Her stomach tightened. With trepidation, she tapped the answer button.

"Hello, Jexi speaking."

"Mrs. Bennett, this is Debbie from Dr. Jeffrey's office," the woman said. "We have the results from your biopsy. The mass came back as benign, but because of its location, the doctor still wants to remove it."

Jexi sucked in a sharp breath. "Benign? Are you sure?"

"Yes, ma'am," Debbie replied. "But there are risks of the tumor attaching to your spine and causing further complications. Dr. Jeffrey would like to get it out of there."

"Okay . . ." Jexi said cautiously. "When? How soon?"

"Dr. Jeffrey has an opening in two weeks."

"Will it be an invasive surgery?" Jexi asked, bracing herself.

"Only a little," Debbie said. "The mass doesn't appear to be interfering with any nerves at this time. So, the doctor will make a small incision, detach the mass, and sew you back up. Since it's near your spine, it could require a short hospital stay, but we won't know until the surgery is complete."

"Alright," Jexi said. "I guess it doesn't sound like I have much of a choice."

"You do have a choice," Debbie said gently, "but if you decline the surgery, the mass might grow onto your spine, and that would create worse issues than you have right now. The surgery then would be much more complicated."

"Well, then . . . let's get this one scheduled," Jexi said.

After the date, time, and location were confirmed, Debbie added, "I'll call you the day before your operation to give you pre-op instructions. Take care."

Jexi ended the call and drew a deep, shaky breath. Relief and fear tangled in her chest. *Benign* was the word she'd prayed for, but surgery still loomed large. She immediately hit Hunter's speed dial and told him everything. When she finished with him, she called Shaya.

Once those calls were made, she dialed her parents. As the phone rang, she whispered to herself, "Do not cry. Do not cry. Do not cry."

Her mother answered. "Jexi! Hi, honey!"

Jexi burst into tears, the words tumbling out in a garbled mess.

"Jexi, what's wrong?" her mother asked urgently. "Did you get bad test results?"

"Noooo," Jexi wailed. "My test results were fine. The tumor is benign."

"So," her mom began gently, "those are happy tears?"

"Noooo," Jexi sobbed. "I have to have surgery!"

"Oh, honey," Louise said, her voice softening. "I'm so sorry. Will it be a difficult surgery?"

"Noooo," Jexi wailed again, twisting a tissue in her fingers until it was nearly in shreds.

"Well then what is it, sweetheart?" her mother asked. "What's really wrong?"

Jexi's shoulders sagged. "I'm just . . . scared," she whispered.

Louise chuckled softly. "Oh, honey. Your dad and I will be there. Hunter and Shaya will be there. And most importantly, God will be there. You are going to be fine."

"You're coming?" Jexi asked, sniffing hard.

"Of course we are," Louise replied. "We're going to park the RV at the campground for a few months so we can help you through this."

Jexi cried even harder. "I love you, Mom."

"I love you too, sweetie," Louise said. "You're going to be okay. We're praying for you, and we'll see you soon."

After she disconnected the call, Jexi buried her face in her hands and let the tears come freely. When they finally slowed, she wiped her eyes, blew her nose, and reached for her Bible.

"Lord, help me feel Your peace," she whispered. "I know I shouldn't be afraid, but I am."

She flipped through the pages until she landed in Mark, chapter five—the story of the woman who had suffered for twelve long years. Isolated, shunned, and desperate, the woman had reached out and touched the hem of Jesus' robe, believing that even that small act of faith would heal her.

Jexi's eyes widened when she reached verse thirty-four. *"Daughter, your faith has healed you. Go in peace and be freed from your suffering."*

Her heart swelled with calm. "Thank You, Father, for meeting me right where I am," she prayed. "I know my life is in Your hands. Not my will, but Yours be done. In Jesus' name, Amen."

She pulled out a notebook and began making a list of everything that needed to be done before surgery: staffing schedules, inventory, bills, advertising. With each item she wrote down, the chaos in her mind quieted a little more.

The shrill ring of the office phone made her jump. She picked it up quickly. "Baxter's Books, this is Jexi. How may I help you?"

"Hello, Jexi!" Shaun said brightly. "I was just reviewing the numbers. Sales have been steadily climbing. Keep up the great work."

"Hi, Shaun!" she replied, her voice steadier than it had been all day. "The store is doing really well. My part-time employees have been incredible, and the advertising is paying off. Renting out the event space has been a huge win. People come in for an event and leave with armfuls of books."

"That's what I like to hear," Shaun said. "I knew that store would be in capable hands!"

"Um . . . speaking of capable hands," Jexi said, hesitating, "those hands are going to need some time off in a couple of weeks. I'm having surgery and I'll be laid up for a bit. I'm not sure how long yet."

"Surgery?!" Shaun exclaimed. "Are you okay?"

"Technically, yes," Jexi replied. "I have a benign tumor in my back, and the doctor wants it out before it grows onto my spine. You know how doctors are."

"I agree with the doctors," Shaun said firmly. "If there's a chance of risk, it needs to be removed."

"Well, since I won't be able to work for a while, I was hoping to have my employees take on a few extra hours. I just wanted to clear that with you since you handle payroll."

"I'll not hear of it!" Shaun barked.

"Oh . . . okay then," Jexi began, panic fluttering in her chest.

"I mean I won't hear of *you* worrying about that," Shaun clarified. "I have plenty of capable hands here. I'll take care of the bookstore in your absence. Frankly, I need to check on my investment anyway. I can stay at least a week, and after that I'll approve whatever hours your staff needs. What day is your surgery?"

Jexi let out a breath she hadn't realized she was holding. "That is incredibly kind of you, Shaun. It's scheduled for July sixth; two weeks from now. Thank you so much."

When the call ended, she glanced at the clock. Paige and Brian would be in within the hour, and Krista was already working the floor. The last thing on her list today was to tell them the news.

"Hey, Krista," Jexi called, her voice echoing softly through the store. "Can you come in here for a moment?"

Krista appeared in the doorway a few seconds later. "Yes, boss?" she asked with a curious smile.

Jexi scoffed. "You don't have to call me *boss*," she said gently. "But I need to talk to you. Have a seat." She motioned toward the chairs across from her desk.

Krista hesitated. "Am I in trouble?"

"No, no, nothing like that," Jexi assured her quickly. "I'm going to be having surgery soon, and I'll need you to step up and take care of a few more things around here while I recover. Would you be open to learning some of the administrative duties?"

"Surgery?" Krista's eyes widened.

"Yes, but it's nothing too serious," Jexi said with a reassuring smile. "I'll explain everything once Paige and Brian get here. For now, I just wanted to ask if you'd be willing to help with the bookkeeping and a few management tasks."

Krista straightened in her chair, determination settling in. "Of course! Whatever I can do to help."

Jexi felt her throat tighten. She hadn't realized how much she needed to hear that. "Thank you, Krista. This place means a lot to me, and knowing you're willing to help carry it for a little while . . . it takes a huge weight off my shoulders."

Krista reached across the desk and gave her hand a quick squeeze. "You just focus on getting better. Baxter's Books will still be standing when you come back."

Jexi smiled, blinking back tears. "With a team like you, Paige, and Brian," she said softly, "I know it will be."

CHAPTER THIRTY-FOUR

The next few months flew by with a flurry of activity. Jexi recovered from surgery and gradually returned to work. She felt better than ever and was truly enjoying her time at the bookstore again. She and Hunter made a point to spend two or three evenings together each week, and their marriage felt renewed. She was also soaking up every moment with her parents, knowing how much she would miss them when they hit the road again. Some evenings, as she sat quietly with her Bible open in her lap, she found herself overwhelmed with gratitude for how blessed her life had become.

Meanwhile, Shaya and Ben poured their hearts into preparing for the baby. They decorated the nursery with a Bible story theme. The blue walls were adorned with Noah and the ark, David standing bravely before Goliath, Jesus welcoming children, the good Samaritan kneeling beside a wounded stranger. Nearly every night they stood in the center of that little room, hands joined, praying for the baby boy who would soon change their lives. They prayed for Selena's delivery, for the baby's health, for wisdom as parents, and above all that, God's will would be done.

By October, Selena's due date was drawing close. Her first semester of online classes was going well, and she was set to begin nursing school in January. Therapy was helping her face the trauma left behind by her boyfriend in Honduras, and she was learning how to prepare her heart for the day she would place her baby in Shaya and Ben's arms.

One evening she stood before the mirror, turning slowly from side to side, marveling at how large her belly had grown. A flicker of worry crossed her mind. Would her body ever feel the same again? But the thought faded just as quickly. She laid her hand over the place where her son pressed gently against her skin and smiled.

No matter what came next, her baby would be deeply, fiercely loved.

She heard Jessie call from the kitchen. "Selena! Lunch is ready!"

Selena shuffled in and the two sat down to grilled cheese sandwiches and tomato soup. Jessie reached for her hand and bowed her head.

"Lord, we thank You for this food. We are grateful for all the blessings You have bestowed upon us. Please help Selena as she gives birth and then transitions into nursing school. Use her to touch lives and accomplish Your will. In Jesus' name, Amen."

Selena took a few bites of soup and felt her stomach churn. She rubbed her swollen belly. "I don't think the baby likes the soup," she giggled.

Jessie smiled. "Babies do have minds of their own."

"Ahhh," Selena groaned suddenly. "The baby *really* doesn't like the soup."

Jessie set her spoon down slowly. "Darlin', that might be more than lunch disagreeing with him. Is it discomfort . . . or pain?"

"Pain. Definitely pain." Selena bent forward, clutching her stomach. "It feels like my insides are being squeezed."

"SHOWTIME!" Jessie shouted. "That baby is on his way!"

Selena grimaced. "How can you be so sure? I've had pains before. You said they were Braxton Hicks. Or gas."

"Does it hurt like it did then?"

"No," Selena groaned. "It's worse."

"Then it's showtime," Jessie declared. "Grab your bag. I'll call Ben and Shaya to meet us at the hospital."

Selena stood and immediately doubled over. "Owwwww!"

"Never mind," Jessie said briskly. "You get yourself to the car. I'll get your bag."

Selena waddled outside and eased into the passenger seat just as another wave of pain rolled through her. Jessie came flying out moments later, purse and hospital bag in hand, already on the phone.

"It's happening!" she yelled. "Selena is having the baby! Get to the hospital, now!"

An hour later, Selena was hooked up to an IV, monitors strapped around her belly, crunching ice chips between contractions. The door flew open and Ben and Shaya rushed in.

"Did we miss him?" Shaya gasped. "They wouldn't let us come to your room until just now!"

Selena managed a smile. "Not yet. The doctor says it'll probably be today, though. My contractions are getting closer."

Ben sank into a chair; his head bowed in silent prayer. Shaya hurried to Selena's side and clasped her hand.

"I'm glad you're here," Selena whispered, squeezing her fingers as another contraction began to build.

"Me too," Shaya said softly. "Is there anything you need? Anything I can get you?"

Selena shook her head. "No, thank you. Jessie has been an incredible nurse." She managed a tired grin.

The next few hours crawled by. They filled the time with prayer, quiet conversation, and speculation about what the baby might look like. Hunter and Jexi arrived and settled into the waiting room, soon joined by Attie, Rance, Aunt Katie, and Uncle Joe.

A powerful contraction tore through Selena.

The nurse checked the monitor and smiled. "This is it! Time to push!"

The room erupted into motion. Machines beeped, gloved hands prepared trays, and the doctor stepped in with an encouraging grin. "I hear we're ready to have a baby today."

Selena clutched Shaya's hand and pushed. Minutes felt like hours, though only twenty-five passed. Finally, she sagged back against the pillows, shaking. "I can't do this anymore," she whispered. "I'm so tired."

"Yes, you can," Shaya said firmly, squeezing her hand. "You are so close. Just a few more."

The nurse nodded. "Two good pushes, sweetheart. That's all you need."

Selena closed her eyes, waited for the cue, and gave everything she had.

A cry sliced through the room.

"Is he here?" Selena gasped. "Is he okay?"

The doctor beamed, lifting the tiny, wriggling baby into view. "You did it. A healthy baby boy."

Tears flowed freely as the nurses cleaned him. Shaya wrapped Selena in a careful hug. "Thank you," she whispered through sobs. "Thank you for this gift."

After a final exam, the doctor smiled again. "Delivery was smooth as silk. You did beautifully. Congratulations, Mama."

The nurse returned, cradling the baby and moving toward Shaya. Shaya raised a hand and turned to Selena.

"Would you like to hold him first?"

Selena shook her head gently, her eyes shining. "No. His mother should hold him first."

Shaya broke down in fresh tears as the nurse placed the baby carefully into the crook of her arm. Ben slipped an arm around her shoulders, and together they stared at the tiny miracle between them.

"Thank You, God," Ben whispered, brushing a finger across the baby's soft forehead.

Inside, Selena was torn in two. The ache her therapist had warned her about washed over her in a sudden wave that was sharp, real, overwhelming. And yet, layered over the grief was an unexpected joy at seeing her son cradled by the parents who would raise him. *This is God's will,* she reminded herself, even as tears blurred her vision.

Jessie cleared her throat gently. "So, Mom and Dad . . . what is this little man's name?"

Shaya wiped her face and smiled through trembling lips. *"Maximiliano,"* she said. Then she turned to Selena. "We want to honor his heritage, your heritage, by giving him a name from Honduras. *Maximiliano Joseph.* We'll call him *Max."*

Selena sniffed, nodding. "Thank you. I couldn't have wished for a better family for him." Her voice softened as she looked at the baby. "Little Max . . . you are going to have such an amazing life."

Jessie hurried to the waiting room and threw the door open. "Maximiliano Joseph Thatcher has arrived!"

The hallway exploded with cheers, hugs, and whispered prayers of gratitude. Jessie raised her hands to quiet them. "Selena and the baby are doing perfectly. God is so good!"

CHAPTER THIRTY-FIVE

Two months later, on a cold December morning, Ben and Shaya stood on the church stage, dedicating their precious son to God. Pastor Dave addressed the congregation.

"Proverbs, chapter twenty-two, verse six, tells us, *'Start children off on the way they should go, and even when they are old, they will not turn from it.'* Today, Ben and Shaya are bringing their son before the Lord, promising to guide him in His ways." He turned toward the congregation. "Will you, Church, commit to helping them raise their son with godly values? It truly takes a village to guide a child along the right path."

Pastor Dave rested his hand gently on the baby and continued, "There are many ways you can support this family. Through prayer, meeting needs as they arise, babysitting, preparing meals, or simply being present. We cannot neglect our role as the village God has called us to be."

He bowed his head. "Please pray with me."

"Father God, we commit this family to You. Give Ben and Shaya wisdom, patience, and strength as they raise their son. Remind them always to turn to You for guidance. In the presence of these witnesses, they promise to bring their child up according to Your principles, and we as a church dedicate ourselves to supporting them along this journey. May Your will be done on earth as it is in Heaven. In Jesus' name, Amen."

The church echoed, "Amen."

Shaya scanned the familiar faces of family and friends while little Max slept peacefully in her arms. Awe filled her heart as she reflected on God's power and faithfulness. She never could have imagined where her life would lead when she stepped onto that cruise ship with Jexi. Yet here she stood, holding the clearest evidence of God's incredible plan.

Thank You, God, she prayed silently. *For everything.*

Later that afternoon, Attie and Rance hosted a celebration in honor of Max's dedication. Attie had gone all out with decorations, with plenty of help from Jessie and Katie. Light blue balloons and streamers filled the kitchen and living room, and a three-tiered cake, frosted in soft blue and topped with a tiny newborn figurine, sat proudly on the table. Every counter was covered with food.

Family and friends filled Rance and Attie's house for the celebration. Shaya was overjoyed that even her brothers had come with their families. The outpouring of love left her overwhelmed. She knew her makeup was long gone, but she couldn't stop the tears. God's grace and generosity had her completely undone.

Max was passed from arm to arm, handling the chaos like a champ. He smiled as people cooed over him, unfazed by the noise. Ben was the proudest father she had ever seen. Shaya giggled as he moved from group to group, flashing photos of Max as if he were the only baby in the world.

Across the room, Selena sat alone, picking at a cupcake.

Shaya crossed the room and slipped onto the couch beside her. "You doing okay?"

Selena nodded, forcing a smile. "I'm fine."

Shaya studied her. "It's okay to have mixed emotions. I know this has to be hard."

A single tear slipped free. Selena brushed it away. "I don't want to feel jealous. Or sad. I know Max is exactly where he needs to be. When I imagine trying to raise him myself, it doesn't make sense at all. I know we did the right thing." Her voice wavered. "So why does it still hurt?"

Shaya slid an arm around her shoulders. "Because you're human," she said gently. "You carried him for nine months. You brought him into this world. It's okay to love him and miss him."

Selena sniffed. "Really?"

"Really. It would be more concerning if you didn't feel that way. You'll work through it, but it will take time. And remember, you can call us anytime. You can come see Max whenever you want. We aren't keeping him from you."

Selena twisted her hands together. "Do you think I'll have a family of my own someday? When I'm ready?"

Shaya smiled. "I'm almost certain you will. God will bring the right man into your life at the right time. Just keep pursuing Him. You'll be amazed by how He blesses you."

Selena dried her eyes. "I know that it is His will for you to be Max's parents. I will continue to follow Him. He has already blessed me so much."

"Your sacrifice will never be forgotten, and we will pray for you always," Shaya said as she pulled Selena into a warm embrace.

Selena sat back and looked at her. "Thank you, Shaya. Thank you for being so wonderful. Your whole family has been amazing to me, and I am truly thankful."

"We are blessed by you, too," Shaya replied.

Jexi walked over to them. "I hope I'm not interrupting," she said.

Shaya stood and wrapped her in a huge hug.

"Can you believe all this?" Jexi asked. "We had no idea any of this would be in store for us, but here it is. Thank you for pushing me toward Christ. I am forever grateful."

"You're making it weird," Shaya giggled. "But this time, it's okay. I'm grateful for you and all of your support. Besides Ben, there is nobody else I'd want as my best friend."

"Likewise," Jexi said. "Okay, weird moment over."

The girls laughed like they were the only ones in the room.

"What am I missing?" Harli asked as she approached.

Shaya hugged her. "I'm so glad you've moved here. How's house hunting going?"

"Good!" Harli said. "I've narrowed it down to about ten different houses!" She laughed at herself.

Jexi giggled. "Easy choices, huh?"

Harli rolled her eyes. "Yeah. But I know I'll find the right one eventually." She lifted her hand, showing off a sparkling diamond ring. "But Sebastian will have to help make the final decision."

Shaya and Jexi's jaws dropped.

"NO WAY!" Shaya shouted. "I knew it!"

"I'm so excited!" Jexi squealed.

"Yeah, yeah, it's no big deal," Harli said, trying, and failing, to sound casual.

"It's a HUGE deal!" Shaya insisted. "I'm so happy for you!" She paused, looking around the room as if taking inventory of every blessing. "God has been so good to all of us. Mom and Dad are together again, Selena is moving forward with her career, Ben and I have Max, Jexi doesn't have cancer, you and Sebastian are engaged . . . I mean, how much better can it get?"

"How about another baby in the family?" Jexi teased.

Shaya snorted. "I'm not ready for that yet. Max is only two months old!"

Jexi shot her a look. "I wasn't talking about you," she said. Her hand drifted unconsciously to her stomach.

Shaya froze, eyes widening. "Are you serious?"

Jexi nodded.

"Don't play with me, now," Shaya warned.

"No games, I promise," Jexi said.

Shaya screeched so loud the entire room fell silent and turned to stare. "Oops," she muttered, glancing around. "Go on about your business. Nothing to see here." She shot Jexi a look that said everything.

"It's okay," Jexi said. She walked over to Hunter and slipped her hand into his. "Shaya just found out that Hunter and I are going to have a baby."

A collective gasp rippled through the room.

Shaya grabbed Harli's hand and lifted it high. "And there's going to be a wedding in the near future! Isn't this day beautiful?"

The entire group erupted into cheers, clapping and celebrating all that God had done.

Jessie lifted her hands toward heaven. "All praise be to God! You crown the year with Your goodness, and Your paths drip with abundance!"

Jexi and Shaya locked eyes, joy radiating between them. With matching smiles, they both shouted, "AMEN!"

www.ingramcontent.com/pod-product-compliance
Lightning Source LLC
LaVergne TN
LVHW090937080826
845145LV00003B/779

* 9 7 8 1 6 3 3 5 7 4 7 8 6 *